RASHI

The Magic AND THE Mystery

Avigdor Bonchek

Copyright © Avigdor Bonchek
drbonchek@gmail.com
Jerusalem 2015/5775

All rights reserved. No part of this publication may be translated, reproduced, stored in a retrieval system or transmitted, in any form or by any means, electronic, mechanical, photocopying, recording or otherwise, without express written permission from the publishers.

Cover design: Leah Ben Avraham/Noonim Graphics
Typesetting: Raphaël Freeman, Renana Typesetting

ISBN: 978-965-229-779-2

1 3 5 7 9 8 6 4 2

Gefen Publishing House Ltd.
6 Hatzvi Street
Jerusalem 94386, Israel
972-2-538-0247
orders@gefenpublishing.com

Gefen Books
11 Edison Place
Springfield, NJ 07081
516-593-1234
orders@gefenpublishing.com

www.gefenpublishing.com

Printed in Israel

Send for our free catalog

Library of Congress Cataloging-in-Publication Data
Bonchek, Avigdor.
  Rashi : the magic and the mystery : keys to unlocking Rashi's unique Torah commentary / Dr. Avigdor Bonchek.
     pages cm
  Includes bibliographical references and index.
  ISBN 978-965-229-779-2
  1. Rashi, 1040-1105. Perush Rashi 'al ha-Torah – Criticism, Textual. I. Title.
  BS1225.S6B66 2015
  296.1092—dc23
                                        2015006021

בס"ד

שמואל קמנצקי
Rabbi S. Kamenetsky

2018 Upland Way
Philadelphia, PA 19131

Home: 215-473-2798
Study: 216-473-1212

בס"ד אור ליום רביעי וירא

לכב' הרה"ג וכו' הרב ר' נחום אייזענשטיין הכ"מ
ה' יציל'ו מכל רע ומכל פגעים רעים
ויתן בכם כח לפעול ולהרבות כבוד שמ"י.

כדי לצאת ידי חובת י"ב הנני לא"ד לא"ד
ידעתי ר' ר' הקדוש ורבו הפוסק ר' שלמה זלמן
אוירבאך זצלה"ה זכור רוב תועלתו ופולוג
ופלג ו אתי הרב לעצעניק אביו והעתיק
דבריו ממה בשו"ת מנחת שלמה חדש ח"א
סי' ז'.

כמו כן אתו ידו"נ ור' מופלג ובקי ארי' פי'
פוירסט דבר ו בפיו"ל רצ"ז

ובשם ש' לחתים להדיו ולהדייק הדבר שאמר
אדוני מו"ר זצ"ל של פלוני

דושה"ט וכט"ס
שמואל קמנצקי

Contents

Preface	vii
Acknowledgments	ix
Chapter 1 Rashi's Life, Personality and Unique Contributions	1
Chapter 2 Rashi and *Pshat* Interpretation	15
Chapter 3 Rashi's Style in Commentary	29
Chapter 4 Why Does Rashi Translate Familiar Words?	37
Chapter 5 Rashi's Use of Midrash	49
Chapter 6 Rashi's *Dibbur Hamatchil*	73
Chapter 7 Rashi and the Rashbam	81
Chapter 8 Questioning Rashi: An Important Key	95
Appendix Answers to Our Questions	129
References	133
Index of Verses Interpreted	135

Preface

I am confident the reader will find fascinating material in this book. I make that not very modest statement because although I have been a Rashi enthusiast for nearly six decades, what I learned about Rashi in preparing this book has enlightened and fascinated me greatly. It is the researchers from whose discoveries I have drawn who deserve the credit. I was one of the benefactors of their work, as I think the reader will be, as well.

My purpose in writing this book is twofold. One is to introduce Rashi the man, the teacher, the commentator and the consummate *mensch* to as wide an audience as possible. The other purpose is to offer educational techniques to help the student uncover the deeper meanings in Rashi's deceptively simple Torah commentary. To my knowledge these techniques have not been spelled out in print before.

I have written a five-part series of books on Rashi called *What's Bothering Rashi?* Those books examined different Rashi comments on the various parshiyot and demonstrated how to analyze them in depth. The reader of *What's Bothering Rashi?* learned certain principles which derived from the many analyses offered in those books.

The present volume explicitly spells out the principles of analysis and illustrates their use with many examples of Rashi comments. I call this book *Rashi: The Magic and the Mystery* because I consider many of Rashi's oh-so-subtle interpretations to be magical – in that he effortlessly and subtly shows us meanings in the Torah's words that may have escaped us, even after years of study. His commentary is a mystery in that we only discover his true message by probing much below the surface; unless and until we do so, the full message of his comment remains a mystery.

Rashi's commentary is a product of the man. One sees in it a reflection of Rashi as a person – his values, his character, his love of Torah and of his fellow Jews. For that reason I have included a brief biography of Rashi and a discussion of his personality, values and approach to halacha.

The major portion of the book deals with Rashi's approach to Torah commentary. I hope to convey something of its uniqueness, its brilliance and its profundity.

In addition, the book is meant to teach and impart to the student the tools necessary for attaining a fuller understanding of Rashi's work. For this reason I have included several "unanswered" questions in the body of the text for the reader to answer himself. I have added an appendix in which I supply suggested answers to these questions.

It is my belief that the student will find in this book helpful insights and guidelines for the study of Rashi, which cannot be found elsewhere.

Avigdor Bonchek
Tishrei 5775
Jerusalem

Acknowledgments

In writing this book, there are many people to whom I am indebted.

I started this book soon after I had undergone a serious operation. My daily schedule was monitored and I was assisted around the clock by my devoted wife, Shulamis. She nursed me back to health and encouraged me all along the way in getting this book finished. I am indebted to her and thankful to her for all the help she has given me all the years of our blessed marriage.

On the academic side, I owe a profound debt of gratitude to Professor Ed Greenstein of Bar-Ilan University, who read the manuscript thoroughly and guided me with his questions and suggestions. I am not a formal student of his and I consider what he did and the time he spent on this work a true act of *chesed*.

For all my books on *parshanut*, Nechama Leibowitz, ע"ה, has been my guiding light, my inspiration and my motivation. Nechama never saw these works and I can only hope that she would have approved of them had she seen them.

Of course, neither Nechama nor, *yibadel me'chaim l'chaim*, Professor Greenstein bear responsibility for the quality of the final product. That of course is my burden and mine alone.

I also am indebted to those who helped me on the financial side of publishing. Among them are my longtime friends, Yitzchak and Barbie Siegel of Silver Spring, MD, and Jackie and

Bruria Siegel of Los Angeles. Dr. and Mrs. Lawrence Bryskin of NYC were kind enough to offer unsolicited assistance. To all of them and to those who chose to remain anonymous, I humbly say thank you.

As always and in all ways, I thank הקדוש ברוך הוא for giving me the opportunity and the health to make my contribution to the beautiful and inexhaustible world of Torah study.

Chapter 1

Rashi's Life, Personality and Unique Contributions

The magic spell cast by Rashi on the Jewish nation over eight centuries ago is still with us. It continues to enlighten and enchant us. His Talmud and Torah commentaries are studied enthusiastically today by more students than in any previous generation. Before we explore the reasons for this, let us first briefly review Rashi's life and the kind of person he was.

The name Rashi is actually an acronym for **Ra**bbi **Sh**lomo son of **Yi**tzchak. He was born in Troyes in north-central France in 1040 CE. He lived in Troyes most of his life, and died there in 1105. He came from a distinguished Torah family. His uncle on his mother's side was Rabbi Shimon the Elder, who learned by Rabbeinu Gershom "light of the exile" (c. 960–1040) in Mainz, Germany. Rashi's father was a Torah scholar; Rashi quotes his father in his commentary to tractate *Avoda Zara* (75a).

Rashi married at about the age of sixteen, then left Troyes to study Torah in nearby Germany where there were some established yeshivot. He first studied in Mainz, where his main teachers were Rabbi Yaakov ben Yakar and Rabbi Yitzchak ben Yehuda. After Rabbi Yaakov died Rashi moved to the yeshiva in Worms, where he studied predominantly under Rabbi Yitzchak ben Eliezer Halevi. Rashi's years of Torah study as a married man in Germany were very difficult ones for him; he lived in dire poverty.

After eight years of studying with these teachers, Rashi moved back home to Troyes. He was soon appointed to the local *beit din* and a few years later, at the age of thirty (in 1070), he opened his own yeshiva.

The following heartfelt panegyric was expressed by a modern-day academic scholar. I quote it at length because we should all share such wonderment and admiration:

> Rashi died in the year 1105. Within a century of his death, his Hebrew commentaries on the Bible and Talmud had spread from the communities of France and Germany to Spain and Africa, to Asia and Babylon. Considering the enormous expense and the mighty energies entailed in the production of hand-copied books, the high cost of paper and parchment, and the great difficulties and obstacles encountered in their distribution in the eleventh and twelfth centuries, the early popularity of Rashi, and the wide and unprecedented dissemination that his commentary on the Bible achieved, are nothing short of remarkable.
>
> The first dated Hebrew printed book comes from Reggio di Calabria in Italy in 1475, and it is Rashi's commentary on the Torah. The first Hebrew printed book from the Iberian Peninsula was the same.... Again, the first Hebrew text of the Pentateuch, printed in 1482, was accompanied by Rashi's commentary. *It may quite safely be asserted that, in the entire history of the written, let alone printed, word, no other commentary on the Hebrew Scriptures in any language has ever attained comparable recognition, acceptance, and sustained popularity or similar wide geographic distribution, or ever equaled it in its profound impact on human lives* [emphasis mine]....

> When we contemplate the phenomenon that is Rashi, our spontaneous reaction is wonderment. We stand almost incredulous at the sheer magnitude of his intellectual and literary achievements. In his age of limited sources of night-time illumination, of inefficient means of indoor heating, devoid of the typewriter, fountain pens or ball-point, without means of mechanical copying, unsupported by governmental funding or any institutional financial aid, and at the same time engaged in his scholarly writing only at odd hours stolen from earning a living, he managed to produce his commentaries to practically the entire Hebrew Bible as well as to the Babylonian Talmud. No one before or since can lay claim to a comparable achievement. What shall we say when this vast bulk, produced under these inherently adverse conditions, also features unmatched qualitative excellence in both content and style? We can only marvel at the phenomenon, bow our heads in reverence, and in all humility profess our boundless admiration for the man. (Nahum Sarna, *Studies in Biblical Interpretation* [Philadelphia: JPS, 2000], , pp. 128–129)

Already in his lifetime Rashi became known for his scholarship throughout northern Europe and in northern Spain; Torah authorities turned to him from all over northwestern Europe. His responsa reflect his scholarship, his modesty and his deeply felt concern for his fellow Jews.

Rashi's popularity continued undiminished throughout the centuries. As evidence of this, we noted that the first Hebrew book printed after the invention of the printing press (1455) was Rashi's Torah commentary *even without the Torah itself*! The first book printed was the Gutenberg Bible in 1455; but the first Hebrew book was not the Torah, but Rashi's commentary on it, in 1475!

I would add just one more indication of Rashi's exclusive place among Torah commentators. No one refers to Rashi as "the Rashi." All other commentators are often referred to with the definitive article – *the* Ramban, *the* Ibn Ezra, *the* Rashbam. The definitive article identifies one among many. But Rashi needs no definitive identification – he is known by all!

Rashi: Creator of New Words

Another one of Rashi's unique contributions to Jewish culture is rarely mentioned. It is Rashi's creation of new Hebrew words – estimated at over a thousand in number! Rashi almost certainly did not use Hebrew as his lingua franca and he probably did not even teach in Hebrew in his yeshiva, yet nevertheless all his writings were in Hebrew. This is in contrast to the Spanish *rishonim* who often wrote Torah books in Arabic. Rashi's familiarity with Hebrew was superior. Yitzchak Avineri published two thick volumes (*Heichal Rashi*, 1979, 1985) on the subject of words that Rashi created. Among them are common and basic words such as *parshan* (commentator), Yahadut (Judaism) and *haskama* (agreement).

Rashi's Outstanding Personality Traits

Rashi's modesty and humility are legendary. This is evident both in his Torah commentaries and in his real-life dealings with others.

Regarding both honesty and modesty, Rashi excelled as few others do – he publicly admitted his mistakes. In his *teshuvot* he wrote regarding his comment on Yechezkel 40:17: "I erred in this comment." It is exceedingly rare to hear a scholar, then or now, reveal such fallibility. Yet this was not a one-time thing for Rashi.

Avraham Grossman has pointed out an interesting and

revealing aspect of Rashi's comments.* Grossman illustrated how Rashi, when describing a righteous person either in Tanach or in the Talmud, always emphasized the individual's modesty. For example, the Torah states: נח איש צדיק, תמים היה בדורותיו, "Noach was a righteous person, *tamim* in his generation" (Bereishit 6:9). The Talmud (*Avoda Zara* 6a) discusses the meaning of the word תמים and concludes that it means תמים בדרכיו, perfect in his ways. On this, Rashi comments: עניו ושפל רוח, "Modest and of lowly spirit." The Talmud itself makes no mention of modesty but Rashi inserts this, implying that modesty is the obvious meaning of being "perfect in one's ways."

Another example (of many) from the Talmud comes from tractate *Berachot* (9b). The Talmud mentions the concept of ותיקין, men who prayed at sunrise. Rashi explains the term ותיקין as אנשים ענוים ומחבבין מצוה, "modest men who love the mitzvot." Note that the Talmud there makes no mention of modesty, but Rashi did – because in his eyes this was a basic trait of good people.

Rashi's modesty is apparent in his real-life dealings with his students, his fellow Jews and his teachers.

E.M. Lifschitz, in his biography of Rashi, writes:

> His way was always to speak as a student before his teacher, as one who offers his opinion and reasoned advice. He was wont to say, "It is not worth asking me this...," "Who am I to take on this matter?" When appropriate, he would always admit having made a mistake, never hesitating to say, "Until now I had considered this permissible; now I realize I was mistaken." He was not embarrassed to say, "I had not heard that" or "I did not know." (E.M. Lifschitz,

---

* *Rashi* (Jerusalem: Zalman Shazar, 2006, Hebrew), p. 222.

Rashi [Jerusalem: Mossad Harav Kook, 1976, Hebrew], p. 28)

What is striking about Rashi's natural modesty is that it was not due to low self-regard, which is often related to personal insecurities. Rashi could, if he thought it was warranted, abandon all modesty and act assertively; at times he would even argue with his teachers, whom he held in the highest regard. Below is part of his *teshuva* concerning a disagreement he had with his teacher, Rabbi Yitzchak ben Eliezer of Worms:

> Ever since I have come to understand the Talmudic passage involved, my heart has sided with those who permitted. I built up argument upon argument before my teacher but he rejected them all, though he could not produce any proof in support of his opinion. I, on the other hand, had many reasons for my leniency and have substantiated them. However, he did not accept these reasons and I continued arguing before him....and will continue to do so until he will agree with me, just as happened in another case where he came to agree with me in the end. (Israel Elfenbein, *Teshuvot Rashi* [New York: Shulsinger Bros., 1943], p. 130, *teshuva* 103)

In another disagreement with his teachers, this time about the *kashrut* of a slaughtered sheep due to a question about its lungs, Rashi declared the sheep to be kosher against the opinion of his teachers. Rashi explained his position to his son-in-law Rabbi Meir (the Rashbam's father):

> I, your loved one, am informing you that I have not retracted and shall not retract [my halachic decision]. The words of my teachers are not acceptable to me. They replied in a superficial manner. Nevertheless, I am communicating my

words only to a few people. I base my words on the great authority of Rabbi Yaakov ben Yakar. They have not based their ruling on tradition, nor even on Talmudic arguments, but solely on their personal judgment. If they will reply to me in a convincing manner I will retract my decision, but it is difficult for me to cause financial loss to my people. For a variety of reasons it is clear and proper that one should be lenient in this matter. (Elfenbein, p. 57, *teshuva* 59)

Below is another example of Rashi's halachic decisions which went "against the stream" but were certainly based on halachic precedents. The laws regarding wine were of concern to Jews in northern France because many were engaged either in producing or in selling wine. The basic law from the Talmud is that wine touched by an idol worshiper makes it unfit for a Jew. Rabbis – including Rashi's teacher Rabbi Yitzchak ben Yehuda, the *rosh yeshiva* of the famed Mainz yeshiva – had decided that bottled wine had to have two seals on it to protect it from becoming forbidden should a Christian touch it. Rashi wrote to his teacher Rabbi Yitzchak:

> In our place [France] the earlier rabbis had the custom of using one seal [when sending wine to other cities] and among them were great wise men. For ten or fifteen years we have been strict with ourselves [requiring two seals], but the matter is very difficult because the highways are problematic and Jews do not travel on them, and we don't have wine for Kiddush and Havdala and must import it from distant places....
>
> [Rashi therefore concluded that] gentiles in our times are not knowledgeable regarding oblations for idols and are as a one-day-old infant whose touch [of wine] is not forbidden. (Avraham Grossman, *Rashi*, p. 43)

Rashi followed the rule that he himself laid out in his commentary on the Talmudic statement that "the power of leniency is greater" (*Beitza* 2b):

> It is better for [a decisor] to teach us the strength of those who permit, for he relies on his tradition and is not afraid to permit. The strength of those who forbid is no indication [of their greatness], for anyone can forbid things – even things that are in actuality permissible.

This attitude was central to Rashi's halachic thinking.

Rashi's Personal Behavior

In his personal behavior as well as in his halachic decisions, Rashi manifested his sensitivity and concern for his fellow Jews.

Rashi was invited to his teacher's daughter's wedding. There he found himself in a ticklish situation. There is a law that if the hindquarters of a kosher animal is to be eaten, it must be porged in accordance with a strict procedure – stripped of veins, *cheilev* (fat and suet) and sinews. But as the food was being prepared, Rashi noticed that the fat had not been removed – meaning the meat was not kosher.

Rashi himself describes his dilemma:

> My teacher was busy with other matters and he did not notice the omission. I was hesitant about how I should react. If I corrected the oversight, I would be assuming authority in the presence of my teacher. If, however, I did not correct it, a transgression would have been committed. I therefore presented the matter in the form of an inquiry and I asked my teacher, "Is the fat of the thigh muscle of an animal forbidden or not?" He replied: "Certainly it is forbidden." And he immediately gave instructions to porge

the thigh of the deer as is required by law. (Elfenbein, p. 20, *teshuva* 25)

We see how Rashi gracefully resolved this dilemma – he was careful not to embarass his teacher and while not avoiding the matter completely, he brilliantly achieved his goal without assuming authority inappropriately.

Rashi's concern for the feelings of others brought him to do things that others could interpret as going against the halacha.

Once, in Rashi's community, there was a funeral during *chol hamoed*. While funerals are carried out during *chol hamoed*, other laws of mourning are not observed. In such cases the mourning period begins after the *chag*. At the funeral many were opposed to reciting Kaddish or Tzidduk Hadin. Nevertheless, Rashi got up and said both Tzidduk Hadin and Kaddish. After the funeral the family should not have sat shiva but, perhaps unaware of the law, they did. Rashi went to the house to comfort the mourners, for he knew that refraining from doing so would add more sorrow to their already burdensome tragedy.*

During Rashi's lifetime, Christians had succeeded in converting numerous Jews. Many of the Jews who converted did so out of fear or for economic or social reasons, rather than out of genuine belief. Rabbeinu Gershom, the rabbinic leader of the generation preceding Rashi, had made very strict proclamations on this matter: אף על פי שחטא, ישראל הוא – conversion does not absolve a Jew of his Jewishness. Rabbeinu Gershom even said that anyone who spoke badly about a convert who returned to Judaism by reminding him of his previous conversion should be excommunicated. Rashi applied this attitude in many halachot. To cite one such example, Rashi was asked to rule regarding a *kohen*

---

* Elfenbein, *Teshuvot Rashi*, , pp. 209–210.

who had converted to Christianity and then returned to the fold. Rashi decreed: "He is permitted to say the Priestly Blessing and receive the first aliya to the Torah."*

Rashi's Torah commentary reflects his love of peace as well. In parashat Bechukotai the Torah recounts the blessings G-d will bestow upon His people when they observe the mitzvot:

VAYIKRA 26:5–6

וְהִשִּׂיג לָכֶם דַּיִשׁ אֶת־בָּצִיר וּבָצִיר יַשִּׂיג אֶת־זָרַע וַאֲכַלְתֶּם לַחְמְכֶם לָשֹׂבַע וִישַׁבְתֶּם לָבֶטַח בְּאַרְצְכֶם: וְנָתַתִּי שָׁלוֹם בָּאָרֶץ...

Your threshing will last until vintage and the vintage will last until the sowing; you will eat your bread to satiety, and you will dwell securely in your land. *I will provide peace in the land....*

RASHI, VAYIKRA 26:6

ונתתי שלום: שמא תאמרו, "הרי מאכל, והרי משתה", אם אין שלום אין כלום... מכאן שהשלום שקול כנגד הכל.

I will provide peace in the land: Maybe you will say, "There is food, there is drink," *but if there is no peace there is nothing... for peace is equal to everything.*

In parashat Noach we learn of the generation of the Flood, who were destroyed because of their looting and sexual transgressions. Later we learn that those who tried to defy G-d by building the Tower of Babel were punished by being dispersed throughout the world. Rashi comments:

RASHI, BEREISHIT 11:9

וכי אי זו קשה, של דור המבול או של דור הפלגה? אלו לא פשטו יד בעיקר, ואלו פשטו יד בעיקר כביכול להלחם בו, ואלו נשטפו, ואלו לא נאבדו מן העולם!

---

* Lifschitz, *Rashi*, p. 32.

אלא שדור המבול היו גזלנים והייתה מריבה ביניהם לכך
נאבדו, ואלו היו נוהגים אהבה וריעות ביניהם, שנאמר שפה
אחת ודברים אחדים. למדת ששנוי המחלוקת וגדול השלום.

Who were worse – the generation of the Flood or the generation of the Dispersion? [The generation of the Flood] did not rebel against G-d, while [the generation of the Dispersion] did rebel; yet [the generation of the Flood] were destroyed while [the generation of the Dispersion] were not killed!

This is because they [of the Flood] did evil to each other, so they were destroyed, while they [of the Dispersion] showed love toward one another so they were saved. This teaches us that *fights are hateful, and peace is great.*

Rashi's preoccupation with peace among people and his concern for the feelings of others finds expression in his commentary, in his halachic decisions and in his personal behavior. This indicates how thoroughly these values were interwoven into his very being.

Rashi's Approach to Creative Torah Education

As we said at the outset, the name Rashi is an acronym of the letters *resh*, *shin* and *yud* which stand for his full name, **Rabbi Shlomo Yitzchaki**. Because of Rashi's success in educating the Jewish people, these letters have been given an additional meaning – **Rabban Shel Yisrael** – the Teacher of Israel. This is obviously so, when we consider that Rashi's running commentary on the Talmud made that difficult Aramaic text accessible to people who could never have fathomed it otherwise. Likewise, his Torah commentary has taught and inspired generation after generation to love and understand our basic text – the Torah.

When Rashi returned to his hometown, Troyes, after studying in the German yeshivot, he opened up his own *beit midrash* (yeshiva). The contributions of Rashi's many well-known students are attributed to *beit midrasho shel Rashi* – Rashi's *beit midrash*. This is not a physical structure – it is a concept. It refers to all those Torah scholars after Rashi who taught Torah using his analytical approach. This includes a wide array of scholars; to name a few – the authors of the Tosephot commentaries on the Talmud, Rav Yoseph Kara, the Rashbam, Rav Simcha of Vitri and the Rivan. Rashi's students composed commentaries on Talmud, Tanach and Midrash, and wrote books on a wide variety of topics – including Hebrew grammar, Jewish history, prayer customs, halachic *teshuvot* and even astronomy.

One wonders: How did Rashi succeed in inspiring so many students to engage in such a variety of creative activity? It seems that the magic flowed naturally from Rashi's personality, his love of his students and his approach to learning.

We have mentioned Rashi's instinctive humility. Rashi referred to his students as *"chaverim"* (friends), and *"chavivai"* (my beloved ones). He treated his students as equals, accepted their criticisms with sober respect and encouraged them to think independently. As we have seen, Rashi argued unabashedly with his own teachers and he encouraged his students to do the same, when appropriate. This open, free atmosphere is fertile ground for creativity; when a student is not afraid to voice his ideas, he gives them free reign. If, conversely, a student fears reproach for what might be seen as a "silly" idea, he becomes hesitant to ever express himself.

This concept, though basic to good education, is unfortunately rare even in our modern, "enlightened" day.

Grossman has pointed out an interesting Talmudic passage which expresses this point exquisitely.* The Talmud (*Sanhedrin*

---

* Avraham Grossman, *Emunot v'Dei'ot b'Olamo shel Rashi* (Alon Shvut: Tevunot, 2008), p. 31.

41b) tells of an interchange between Rav Kahana and Rav Safra when they met Rami bar Chama. Rami asked them if they had any *chidushim* in their *beit midrash*. They gave an answer, to which Rami approvingly replied, "If so, you have many [*tuva*] *chidushim* to say." They answered him, "Because you have been good [*tuv*] to us, we have much [*tuva*] to say."

Rashi's comment on these words is striking. He explains this as follows: "Because you are good and *humble* [emphasis mine] and concede to us, we have a lot to say!" Here Rashi has given us, in a nutshell, his secret of success as a teacher. By being "good" to one's students they feel wanted, respected and encouraged to express themselves freely. The rabbis did not use the word *humble* in their answer to Rami; Rashi added it because he viewed humility as an essential characteristic for a good teacher.

Rashi's Children

Rashi was blessed with several daughters – it is unclear whether the exact number was three or four. Two of his daughters, Miriam and Yocheved, married *talmidei chachamim* and both had children who became well-known scholars. Yocheved married Rabbi Meir ben Shmuel; they had four sons and two daughters. Their sons all became rabbinic leaders: Isaac – the Rivam; Samuel – the Rashbam; Solomon the grammarian; and Jacob – Rabbeinu Tam. One of their daughters, Hannah, became a teacher of laws and customs relevant to women. She married Samuel ben Simcha, and their son Isaac of Dampierre – the Ri – became the leading Talmudic scholar of his generation.

Rashi's grandsons carried on after him, heading yeshivot and developing the Tosephot commentaries on the Talmud.

We know that Miriam married Judah ben Nathan (the Rivan) and had a daughter, Alvina, and three sons – Yom Tov, Samson and Eliezer. The sons moved to Paris, where they established a yeshiva. Miriam may have had other daughters whose names are unknown. Miriam is assumed to have died in Troyes, her birthplace, but her date of death is not recorded.

It is believed that Rashi had a third daughter, Rachel, based on a letter by Rabbeinu Tam in which he said she was divorced from Eliezer; they had no children. From various strands of evidence, it is assumed that Rashi had a fourth daughter who died as a young girl; her name is not known.

Chapter 2
Rashi and *Pshat* Interpretation

Rashi's Torah commentary is comprised of both *pshat* and *drash* interpretations. Before we begin a discussion on *pshat* and *drash* within Rashi's commentary, it would be best to define these two terms.

Pshat means interpreting the verse solely on the basis of what it says – and not based on what is assumed, but not said. A central condition for an interpretation to be considered *pshat* is that it fit in with the context – the surrounding verses.

Drash, on the other hand, is not bound either by time or by context. It can refer to things that have not yet occurred and it may make many assumptions of which little hint can be found in the written text. It is, in a sense, a type of "free association" to the words in the verse. There are various types of *drash*; they differ to the degree that they approach *pshat* interpretation, that is, to the extent that they have some anchor in the words of the verse.

The Talmud's Concept of *Pshat*

The following quotation from the Talmud (*Shabbat* 63) indicates that *pshat* interpretation was not that common in Talmudic times. The Talmud discusses whether a man can wear a sword on Shabbat. One opinion is that it is an ornament and thus permissible. The other opinion is that it is a weapon and thus forbidden.

ואמרי לה אביי לרב יוסף: מאי טעמא דר"א דאמר תכשיטין הן לו?

דכתיב (תהלים מה:ד) "חגור חרבך על ירך גבור, הודך והדרך".

א"ל רב כהנא למר בריה דרב הונא: האי בדברי תורה כתיב!

א"ל: אין מקרא יוצא מידי פשוטו.

א"ר כהנא: כד הוינא בר תמני סרי שנין והוה גמירנא ליה לכוליה הש"ס ולא הוה ידענא דאין מקרא יוצא מידי פשוטו עד השתא.

Abaye [asked] R. Yoseph, "What is R. Eliezer's reason for maintaining that they are ornaments for him?"

Because it is written, "Gird your sword upon your thigh, O mighty one, your glory and your majesty" (Tehillim 45:4).

R. Kahana objected to Mar son of R. Huna: "But this refers to the words of the Torah!"

"*A verse cannot depart from its plain meaning (*pshat*),*" he replied.

R. Kahana said, "*By the time I was eighteen years old I had studied the whole* Shas, *yet I did not know that a verse cannot depart from its plain meaning until today.*"

Rashi's contribution in his Torah commentary was in placing emphasis on *pshat*; this signaled a new direction in Torah commentary.

Rashi's Reputation as a *Pshat* Commentator

Rashi is known as a *pshat*-oriented commentator. This assumption stems from Rashi's own statement as to his agenda in his Torah commentary. Rashi did not write an introduction to his Torah commentary, but he briefly stated his agenda in his commentary on Bereishit 3:8. There he writes:

יש מדרשי אגדה רבים וכבר סדרום רבותינו על מכונם בבראשית רבה (יט:ו) ובשאר מדרשות. ואני לא באתי אלא לפשוטו של מקרא ולאגדה המיישבת דברי המקרא דבר דבור על אופניו.

There are many *midrashei aggada* which our rabbis have already organized in *Bereishit Rabba* and the other books of Midrash. But I have only come [to provide] *pshuto shel Mikra* [plain meaning of Scripture] and the *aggada* that serves to clarify the words of Scripture in a way that fits those words.

Rashi's statement has lead many to believe that all of Rashi's commentary is *pshat*. But this is difficult to accept, since we know that about 70 percent of his commentary comes from the Midrash or the Talmud. How can we resolve this problem?

Rashi's statement can be divided into two parts. In his commentary he will 1) interpret according to *pshuto shel Mikra* and 2) also cite those midrashim that fit in with the words of the verse.

So when Rashi says "But I have only come [to provide] *pshat*," he means: "My own personal contributions are my *pshat* interpretations. But I will also cite midrashim if they are not too far removed from the words of the text."

Understanding Rashi's words in this way explains why he cites midrashim despite his commitment to providing a *pshat* commentary. We will see that he will often cite midrashim if his *pshat* interpretation has some weakness to it. We will also see that he rejects using midrashim if they do not have some connection to the words of the verse. Examples of his referral to but rejection of midrashim can be found in Bereishit 3:22, 3:24, 4:8 and 19:15.

Shemot 6:9 is another instance of Rashi offering *pshat* and rejecting a midrashic explanation. Here he explains the reason for his rejection:

ואין המדרש מתיישב אחר המקרא...לכך אני אומר יתיישב המקרא על פשוטו דבור דבור על אופניו, והדרשה תדרש, שנאמר, "הלא כה דברי כאש נאם ה' וכפטיש יפוצץ סלע" (ירמיה כג:כט), **מתחלק לכמה ניצוצות**.

> *But the midrash does not fit well with Scripture's [words].... Therefore I say let the verse be explained according to its* pshat, *fitting its context, and let the* drash *be learned, as it says, "Is not My word as fire, says Hashem, and like a hammer that shatters stone?" (Yirmiyahu 23:29). [So, too, does G-d's word]* divide into many sparks *[i.e., many interpretations].*

In conclusion, Rashi's commentary is not exclusively *pshat*; it is *pshat* with appropriate *drash*.

Below is an example of two comments, one *pshat* and one *drash*, which nevertheless teach the same thing:

SHEMOT 32:5

וַיַּרְא אַהֲרֹן וַיִּבֶן מִזְבֵּחַ לְפָנָיו וַיִּקְרָא אַהֲרֹן וַיֹּאמַר חַג לַה' מָחָר:

And Aharon saw and he built an altar in front of him, and Aharon called and said, "A festival for Hashem tomorrow."

RASHI

וירא אהרן: שהיה בו רוח חיים...

ויאמר חג לה' מחר: לא היום, שמא יבא משה קודם שיעבדוהו, זהו פשוטו. ומדרשו בויקרא רבה (ה:ג): דברים הרבה ראה אהרן. ראה חור בן אחותו, שהיה מוכיחם והרגוהו, וזהו "ויבן מזבח לפניו" – ויבן מזבוח לפניו. ועוד ראה ואמר, "מוטב שיתלה בי הסירחון ולא בהם", ועוד ראה ואמר "אם הם בונים אותו המזבח, זה מביא צרור וזה מביא אבן, ונמצאת מלאכתן נעשית בבת אחת, מתוך שאני בונה אותו ומתעצל במלאכתי, בין כך ובין כך משה בא".

And Aharon saw: That it had the spirit of life....

And he said, "A festival for Hashem tomorrow": Not today. Perhaps Moshe will come before they serve it – that is its pshat interpretation. And the Midrash (Vayikra Rabba 5:3) states: Aharon saw many things. He saw Chur, his sister's son, who reproved them and was killed; that is [the meaning] of "He built an altar before him" – he understood from the slaughter before him. He also saw and said, "Better they should blame me for this transgression and not them." He also saw and said, "If they build the altar this one will bring a stone and this one a rock and the work will be done immediately, but if I build it and go slow with my work, soon Moshe will come."

Let us compare this comment with the following one:

SHEMOT 32:6

וַיַּשְׁכִּימוּ מִמָּחֳרָת וַיַּעֲלוּ עֹלֹת וַיַּגִּשׁוּ שְׁלָמִים וַיֵּשֶׁב הָעָם לֶאֱכֹל וְשָׁתוֹ וַיָּקֻמוּ לְצַחֵק:

And they arose early on the morrow and they brought offerings and peace offerings and the people sat to eat and drink; and they began *to play*.

RASHI

וישכימו: השטן זרזם כדי שיחטאו.
לצחק: יש במשמע הזה גלוי עריות, כמו שנאמר, "לצחק בי" (בראשית לט:יז). ושפיכות דמים, כמו שנאמר, "יקומו נא הנערים וישחקו לפנינו" (שמואל ב' ב:יד). אף כאן נהרג חור.

And they rose early: The Satan rushed them so they should sin.

To play: This refers to illicit sexual relations, as it says, "to mock me [*letzacheik*]" (Bereishit 39:17). And [it refers to] murder, as it says, "Let the lads get up and play in front of us" (2 Shmuel 2:14). [The "play" resulted in the lads killing each other.] Here also [*letzacheik* means that] they killed Chur.

These two Rashi comments from the story of the Golden Calf illustrate an important lesson. On the words in verse 5, "and

Aharon saw," Rashi offers both *pshat* and *drash*. In the *drash* we learn that Chur, Miriam's son, was killed in the uprising. The midrash derives this from the words ויבן מזבח לפניו, which literally mean "and he built an altar in front of him." But the *drash* reads these words otherwise: it understands ויבן to mean "he understood" (from the word להבין – to understand), and it changes the words מזבֵּח לפניו to read מזבוח לפניו – "from the one slaughtered [Chur] in front of him [Aharon]."

This is clearly *drash*.

On verse 6, however, Rashi comments that the word לצחק has several meanings in the Tanach. One is to murder (as seen in 2 Shmuel 2:14); this indicates that Chur was murdered. But according to Rabbi Rafael Pozen – the author of *Parshegen*, a commentary on Targum Onkelos – this is not *drash*; since "murder" is one of the meanings of the word לצחק, the explanation qualifies as *pshat*.

This illustrates how the same conclusion (i.e., that Chur was murdered), which is not mentioned explicitly in the verse, can be reached by both *pshat* and *drash*, depending on how the message is derived from the words of the verse.

The Rashbam's Criticism

The Rashbam, Rashi's grandson, offers us an incredible and unique insight into Rashi's thinking. The following is an excerpt from the Rashbam's comment on verse 37:2 in Bereishit (we will look at the full comment in chapter 7):

> Rabbi Shlomo [Rashi], my mother's father, who illuminated the eyes of the Diaspora, who wrote commentaries on the Torah, the Prophets and the Writings [Tanach], set out to explain the plain meaning of the Scripture. However, I, Shmuel, son of his son-in-law Meir, *zt"l*, often argued

with him and he admitted to me that if only he had had the time, *he would have written new commentaries, based on the insights into the plain meaning of Scripture [*pshat*] that are newly thought of day by day.*

This is a remarkable statement! Rashi tells his grandson (who was probably in his twenties at the time) that he would have rewritten his Torah commentary, if he had had the time, emphasizing more new *pshat* interpretations.

What are we to make of this? Does this mean that the Rashi commentary we have in our printed *chumashim* today is not the best of Rashi? Does it mean that all our efforts to understand the Rashi commentary we have today is an effort in futility, because Rashi himself wished to change what he had written?!

Rashi's comments consist of two interpretive approaches – *pshat* and *drash*. Rashi seems to have been saying that he would have liked to rethink his *drash* interpretations and find new *pshat* interpretations "that are newly thought of day by day." But Rashi's remark does not invalidate his *pshat* interpretations. And it is these "simple" *pshat* comments that are most intriguing and challenging and which require in-depth analysis to uncover his intent. Analysis of Rashi's *pshat* interpretations would thus still need to be done, even if Rashi were to "revise" the *drash* elements in his commentary.

On the other hand, our efforts in understanding Rashi's midrashic comments are attempts to see the connection between the midrash and the text itself. This is always a beneficial endeavor – it helps us better understand the midrash and Rashi as well.

A *Pshat* Interpretation that Rashi Does Not Offer

Let me give an example of Rashi offering a *drash* interpretation where *pshat* might have been appropriate:

BEREISHIT 45:26–28

וַיַּגִּדוּ לוֹ לֵאמֹר עוֹד יוֹסֵף חַי וְכִי־הוּא מֹשֵׁל בְּכָל־אֶרֶץ מִצְרָיִם וַיָּפָג לִבּוֹ כִּי לֹא־הֶאֱמִין לָהֶם: וַיְדַבְּרוּ אֵלָיו אֵת כָּל־דִּבְרֵי יוֹסֵף אֲשֶׁר דִּבֶּר אֲלֵהֶם **וַיַּרְא אֶת־הָעֲגָלוֹת** אֲשֶׁר־שָׁלַח יוֹסֵף לָשֵׂאת אֹתוֹ **וַתְּחִי רוּחַ יַעֲקֹב אֲבִיהֶם**: וַיֹּאמֶר יִשְׂרָאֵל רַב עוֹד־יוֹסֵף בְּנִי חָי אֵלְכָה וְאֶרְאֶנּוּ בְּטֶרֶם אָמוּת:

26) And they told him, saying, "Yoseph is still alive! And he rules over all the land of Egypt." And his heart went faint because he did not believe them. 27) And then they spoke to him, all the words of Yoseph which he had spoken to them, and he *saw the wagons* that Yoseph had sent to transport him *and the spirit of Yaakov their father was revived.* 28) And Israel said, "It is great that Yoseph is still alive; I will go and see him before I die."

The difficulty in this passage is clear. While verse 26 says that Yaakov did not believe the brothers when they reported that Yoseph was alive and was the ruler of Egypt, nevertheless in verse 27 it says Yaakov's spirit was revived, obviously because he now believed them. The question is: What changed? What convinced Yaakov that they were telling the truth?

The commentaries offer various interpretations but none are very convincing. For example, the Rashbam says that Yoseph sent the wagons at Pharaoh's behest (see above 45:19), since there was a law that no wagon could leave Egypt without Pharaoh's approval. The fact that Yaakov saw royal wagons convinced him of the veracity of the brothers' statement about Yoseph being alive. The problem with this interpretation is that the Torah makes no mention of this law or the wagons being royal wagons; *pshat* must be rooted in the words of the Torah. Also our verse says "He saw the wagons that Yoseph had sent to transport him." According to the Rashbam, the verse only had to say: "He saw the wagons that Yoseph had sent," because seeing the wagons was crucial; the words "to transport him" are irrelevant. Why did the Torah add them? These questions weaken the validity of the Rashbam's interpretation.

RASHI, BEREISHIT 45:27

את כל דברי יוסף: סימן מסר להם במה היה עוסק כשפירש ממנו, בפרשת עגלה ערופה. זהו שאמר "וירא את העגלות אשר שלח יוסף" ולא אמר "אשר שלח פרעה".

All the words of Yoseph: [Yoseph] gave them a sign about what [section of Torah study] he had been engaged in when he left [Yaakov] – the chapter of *egla arufa* [the calf whose neck is broken]. That is why it says "And he saw the *agalot* [wagons] that Yoseph had sent," and it didn't say "that Pharaoh had sent."

Rashi's *drash* explanation is that Yaakov saw the wagons (הָעֲגָלוֹת) and this reminded him that before Yoseph disappeared they had been learning together the chapter of עגלה ערופה – the broken-necked calf. In Devarim 20 we read of the procedure done when a dead man is found in a field between two cities and the murderer is unknown. The procedure consists of breaking the neck of a calf – called the עגלה ערופה. The fact that Yoseph sent עֲגָלוֹת was seen by Yaakov as a sign from Yoseph that he was alive, because only Yaakov and Yoseph knew what they had been learning.

Rashi's comment is most certainly *drash* and not *pshat*. There are several indications that this is *drash*: 1) The chapter on עגלה ערופה was only taught at Mount Sinai, several hundred years after Yaakov's time. 2) The two words have different meanings, and even different roots: עֶגְלָה with a *segol* means "calf," whereas עֲגָלָה with a *patach* means "wagon." There is no grammatical connection between the wagons and what Yaakov had purportedly learned with Yoseph.

Our question is: Is there a *pshat* explanation for Yaakov believing his sons soon after the Torah said he didn't believe them? To reach a *pshat* explanation we rely only on what is written and on common sense.

The only verse that separates Yaakov's disbelief from his belief is verse 27. The verse reads:

וַיְדַבְּרוּ אֵלָיו אֵת **כָּל־דִּבְרֵי יוֹסֵף** אֲשֶׁר דִּבֶּר אֲלֵהֶם וַיַּרְא **אֶת־הָעֲגָלוֹת** אֲשֶׁר־שָׁלַח יוֹסֵף לָשֵׂאת אֹתוֹ וַתְּחִי רוּחַ יַעֲקֹב אֲבִיהֶם:

And then they spoke to him, *all the words of Yoseph* which he had spoken to them, *and he saw the wagons* that Yoseph had sent to transport him and the spirit of Yaakov their father was revived.

The verse states that the brothers told Yaakov all the words of Yoseph. What were the words Yoseph had spoken? Earlier in the chapter, Pharaoh commanded Yoseph to tell his brothers: "Take for yourselves from the land of Egypt wagons for your small children and your wives; *transport your father and come*" (Bereishit 45:19). It is clear from this that the brothers told Yaakov that Yoseph had sent the wagons for the purpose of transporting him to Egypt. The verb *nasa*, meaning transport, is purposely used in both verses in order to refresh our memory and remind us of what Yoseph had said about the wagons.

After emphasizing what Yaakov was told, verse 27 focuses on what Yaakov saw: "the wagons that Yoseph had sent to transport him." If the reason Yaakov believed the brothers was, as the Rashbam argued, because only the king would send such royal wagons, then the Torah need not have added the final words "to transport him." But if the convincing point was that Yaakov would now go down to Egypt to see his son, these last words are crucial.

And why was this so convincing? Because it proves that the brothers must be telling the truth about Yoseph. Otherwise what would happen if Yaakov made the arduous trip through the Sinai desert to Egypt and finally got there – but there was no Yoseph?!
Verse 28 solidifies this interpretation:

וַיֹּאמֶר יִשְׂרָאֵל רַב עוֹד־יוֹסֵף בְּנִי חָי אֵלְכָה וְאֶרְאֶנּוּ בְּטֶרֶם אָמוּת:

And Israel said: "It is great that Yoseph is still alive; *I will go and see him before I die.*"

The fact that Yaakov immediately said "*I will go and see him* before I die" clinches it – these words show us that Yaakov's believing was based on his going to see the live Yoseph as soon as possible.

This explanation fulfills the requirement of a *pshat* interpretation – it is totally anchored in the words of the Torah; no outside assumptions are necessary.

Perhaps this is the kind of change Rashi would have made "according to new *pshat* understandings" had he had the time to do so. He would not have had to use a midrash that is far from the Torah's words.

What Does It Mean to Study Rashi In Depth?

Our goal is to understand Rashi's comments *in depth*. What we mean by "in depth" has been precisely defined by Avraham Bakrat, one of the early Sephardi commentaries on Rashi, in his work *Sefer Zikaron* (commentary to Shemot 25:34). He has outlined three levels of interpreting Rashi's comments:

1. Understanding *what* Rashi is saying (i.e., the meaning of his words and of his comment).
2. Understanding *why* Rashi had the need to comment. What was difficult in the verse that, without Rashi's comment,

we would not understand? We call this "What is bothering Rashi?"

3. When Rashi's comment conflicts with other commentaries, we ask: What *evidence* is there that Rashi is correct?

To illustrate the process of studying Rashi's commentary in depth, let us analyze his comment on Shemot 2:23. The verses read:

SHEMOT 2:23–25

וַיְהִי בַיָּמִים הָרַבִּים הָהֵם וַיָּמָת מֶלֶךְ מִצְרַיִם וַיֵּאָנְחוּ בְנֵי יִשְׂרָאֵל מִן הָעֲבֹדָה וַיִּזְעָקוּ וַתַּעַל שַׁוְעָתָם אֶל הָאֱלֹקִים מִן הָעֲבֹדָה: וַיִּשְׁמַע אֱלֹקִים אֶת נַאֲקָתָם וַיִּזְכֹּר אֱלֹקִים אֶת בְּרִיתוֹ אֶת אַבְרָהָם אֶת יִצְחָק וְאֶת יַעֲקֹב: וַיַּרְא אֱלֹקִים אֶת בְּנֵי יִשְׂרָאֵל וַיֵּדַע אֱלֹקִים:

And it was in those many days *and the king of Egypt died* and the Children of Israel groaned from the labor and they cried out and their outcry rose to G-d from the labor. And G-d heard their moaning and G-d remembered His covenant with Avraham, Yitzchak and Yaakov. And G-d saw the Children of Israel and G-d knew.

RASHI, SHEMOT 2:23

וימת מלך מצרים: נצטרע והיה שוחט תינוקות ישראל ורוחץ בדמם.

And the king of Egypt died: He had *tzaraat* and would slaughter Jewish infants and wash himself in their blood.

The first level requires us to simply understand what Rashi is saying. That is easy here. He says that Pharaoh didn't really die; he became sick with *tzaraat* (leprosy) and his unusual and cruel treatment was to wash himself in the blood of murdered Jewish children.

The second level is to understand why Rashi says this. Why doesn't Rashi accept the simple meaning that Pharaoh actually died? Rashi may have been basing himself on the Talmud's statement (*Nedarim* 64b) that one who has *tzaraat* is like a dead person, but being actually dead is certainly more *pshat* than being *"as if dead"* – so why did Rashi prefer the Talmud's statement? Look back at the verses – do you see why?

The answer is that the verse states that the Jews groaned after Pharaoh died! That is strange; one would think they would have rejoiced when this evil man died. This seems to be what bothered Rashi and led to his comment. The Jews groaned because Pharaoh was actually still alive; he was sick and slaughtered many Jewish children – that is why they groaned when he "died."

The third level is to find evidence that this is so, i.e., that Pharaoh did not actually die. The evidence that Rashi is right comes from a little-known fact that the Vilna Gaon discovered. With the exception of our verse, when discussing the death of a king the Tanach never refers to the king by his title. For example when the Tanach speaks of David in his old age it says:

1 MELACHIM 1:1–2

וְהַמֶּלֶךְ דָּוִד זָקֵן בָּא בַּיָּמִים וַיְכַסֻּהוּ בַּבְּגָדִים וְלֹא יִחַם לוֹ: וַיֹּאמְרוּ לוֹ עֲבָדָיו יְבַקְשׁוּ לַאדֹנִי הַמֶּלֶךְ נַעֲרָה בְתוּלָה וְעָמְדָה לִפְנֵי הַמֶּלֶךְ...

And *King* David was old, coming into days; and they covered him with garments but he wasn't warm. And his servants said to him, "Let them seek a young woman for my master the *king* and she will stand before the *king*....

But when David actually died the verse says:

1 MELACHIM 2:10

וַיִּשְׁכַּב דָּוִד עִם־אֲבֹתָיו וַיִּקָּבֵר בְּעִיר דָּוִד:

And David lay down with his fathers; and he was buried in the city of David.

We see that when David died he was no longer referred to as "King David" but simply as "David." This, the Gaon says, is explained in Kohelet (8:8):

וְאֵין שִׁלְטוֹן בְּיוֹם הַמָּוֶת...

There is no rulership on the day of death.

Given this principle, the statement in Shemot 2:23 that the king died cannot be taken literally because the Torah would not refer to him as "king" on the day of his death. This supports Rashi's comment that he didn't really die, but was only stricken with *tzaraat*. This, then, is our third level of in-depth understanding.

We should strive to achieve this level of in-depth understanding when we study Rashi's commentary.

Chapter 3

Rashi's Style in Commentary

Rashi's comments have a certain style to them. His comments are usually short, they usually answer unasked questions and they use precise language to convey his message. In addition to these stylistic characteristics we notice that his comments can be divided into two main types.

For centuries both Ashkenazi and Sephardi teachers have taught their young pupils to critically analyze Rashi's comments by asking one of two possible questions, depending on the type of comment Rashi makes. I call them Type I and Type II comments.

Type I Comment

When a sentence in the Torah presents a difficulty in understanding, such as a contradiction, or if something is not clear or if it is a non sequitur, then Rashi supplies an answer to the difficulty, but without explicitly telling us what the difficulty is. In this case we would ask: "What in the text is bothering Rashi?" Most Rashi comments fall into this category. We will see that even Rashi's midrashic comments are frequently rooted in some problem in the text that is "bothering Rashi."

Some examples will help clarify this. The following comes from G-d's response to Moshe's pleading to forgive the people for the sin of the spies.

BAMIDBAR 14:20–23

וַיֹּאמֶר ה' סָלַחְתִּי כִּדְבָרֶךָ: וְאוּלָם חַי אָנִי וְיִמָּלֵא כְבוֹד ה' אֶת כָּל

הָאָרֶץ: כִּי כָל הָאֲנָשִׁים הָרֹאִים אֶת כְּבֹדִי וְאֶת אֹתֹתַי אֲשֶׁר עָשִׂיתִי בְמִצְרַיִם וּבַמִּדְבָּר וַיְנַסּוּ אֹתִי זֶה עֶשֶׂר פְּעָמִים וְלֹא שָׁמְעוּ בְּקוֹלִי: אִם יִרְאוּ אֶת הָאָרֶץ אֲשֶׁר נִשְׁבַּעְתִּי לַאֲבֹתָם וְכָל מְנַאֲצַי לֹא יִרְאוּהָ:

And Hashem said: "I have forgiven *as you said*. But as I live, the whole earth shall be filled with the glory of Hashem. All the men who have seen My glory and My signs which I have done in Egypt and in the wilderness and have tested Me ten times and have not heeded My voice – surely they will not see the land that I have sworn to their fathers and all My provokers will not see it."

RASHI, BAMIDBAR 14:20

כדברך: בשביל מה שאמרת – "פן יאמרו מבלתי יכולת ה'".

As you said: Because of what you said – "Lest they say: Hashem was not able...."

Rashi here provides an implicit answer to an unstated question. The unstated question is: How could Hashem say He has forgiven when in the next verses He vows to punish those who provoked Him?

Can you think of an answer? (See the appendix, page 129.) Another example of Rashi providing an answer to an unstated question concerns Yaakov's preparations for Esav's arrival.

BEREISHIT 33:2

וַיָּשֶׂם אֶת־הַשְּׁפָחוֹת וְאֶת־יַלְדֵיהֶן רִאשֹׁנָה וְאֶת־לֵאָה וִילָדֶיהָ אַחֲרֹנִים וְאֶת־רָחֵל וְאֶת־יוֹסֵף אַחֲרֹנִים:

And he placed the maidservants and their children first; *and Leah and her children last,* and Rachel and Yoseph last.

RASHI

ואת לאה וילדיה אחרונים: אחרון אחרון חביב.

And Leah and her children last: The further back, the more beloved.

Here too Rashi is bothered by a question, which he does not state openly. His unstated question is: How can the Torah call Leah and her children the last (אחרונים)? She was certainly not the last – Rachel was!

How does his brief comment answer this question? (See the appendix, page 129.)

The vast majority of Rashi comments can be similarly analyzed, even those that are mainly from Midrash. The next Rashi comment illustrates how Rashi will use a midrash to deal with a difficulty in the Torah's words.

BEREISHIT 24:62

וְיִצְחָק בָּא מִבּוֹא בְּאֵר לַחַי רֹאִי וְהוּא יוֹשֵׁב בְּאֶרֶץ הַנֶּגֶב:

And Yitzchak came *from the well Lachai Roi*; and he dwelt in the land of the Negev.

RASHI

מבוא באר לחי ראי: שהלך להביא הגר לאברהם אביו שישאנה.

From the well Lachai Roi: For he had gone to bring Hagar [back] to Avraham his father that he might [re]marry her.

Here Rashi cites a midrash. Why? We must assume that there is some difficulty in the text. We ask: What is bothering Rashi here?

Our answer: The words בא מבוא, which literally mean "came from coming," are strangely redundant. The word מבוא is awkward and unnecessary. It should have said simply, "And Yitzchak came from the well...." The apparently redundant and unusual word מבוא is probably what is bothering Rashi. Therefore, Rashi tells us that the word bears a special message. Here the word מבוא has the sense of "bringing" (להביא in Rashi's comment) and not "coming" as we might have thought. What was Yitzchak bringing? Why Hagar, of course, because she was last seen at this very same well of Lachai Roi (see Bereishit 16:14) and she is next seen as being Avraham's wife following Sarah's death (see Bereishit 25:1 and Rashi's comment there). We now see how Rashi's comment answers the difficulty. There is a certain poetic beauty implied in this *drash*. Just as Avraham was involved in seeking a wife for his son Yitzchak, so too was Yitzchak looking for a wife for his father after his mother Sarah had died.

Most Rashi comments in the Torah are of this Type 1. But, as we said, there is also another type of comment, which we describe below.

Type II Comment

When the Torah sentence is likely to be misunderstood, Rashi will add a word or two and place it between the Torah's words. The purpose of such a brief comment is to prevent students from making a likely error and guide them in the right direction. The appropriate question to ask upon seeing a Rashi comment like this is "What misunderstanding is Rashi warning us about and helping us avoid?" How would I have (mis)understood the Torah's words had Rashi not commented? This type of comment has an identifying style. It usually adds a word or a short phrase between the *dibbur hamatchil* (lead words) and the other words quoted from that verse. Rashi's additional words act as a bridge between the *dibbur hamatchil* and the other Torah words. This is a less frequent type of comment, but it occurs sufficiently frequently that understanding it will be helpful.

An example will show how this type of comment works. The following verses record Yaakov's negotiations with Lavan over his wages:

BEREISHIT 30:31–35

לֹא וַיֹּאמֶר מָה אֶתֶּן־לָךְ וַיֹּאמֶר יַעֲקֹב לֹא־תִתֶּן־לִי מְאוּמָה אִם־תַּעֲשֶׂה־לִּי הַדָּבָר הַזֶּה אָשׁוּבָה אֶרְעֶה צֹאנְךָ אֶשְׁמֹר: **לב** אֶעֱבֹר

בְּכָל־צֹאנְךָ הַיּוֹם הָסֵר מִשָּׁם כָּל־שֶׂה ׀ נָקֹד וְטָלוּא וְכָל־שֶׂה־חוּם בַּכְּשָׂבִים וְטָלוּא וְנָקֹד בָּעִזִּים וְהָיָה שְׂכָרִי: לג וְעָנְתָה־בִּי צִדְקָתִי בְּיוֹם מָחָר כִּי־תָבוֹא עַל־שְׂכָרִי לְפָנֶיךָ כֹּל אֲשֶׁר־אֵינֶנּוּ נָקֹד וְטָלוּא בָּעִזִּים וְחוּם בַּכְּשָׂבִים גָּנוּב הוּא אִתִּי: **לד** וַיֹּאמֶר לָבָן הֵן לוּ יְהִי כִדְבָרֶךָ: **לה** וַיָּסַר **בַּיּוֹם הַהוּא** אֶת־הַתְּיָשִׁים הָעֲקֻדִּים וְהַטְּלֻאִים וְאֵת כָּל־הָעִזִּים הַנְּקֻדּוֹת וְהַטְּלֻאֹת כֹּל אֲשֶׁר־לָבָן בּוֹ וְכָל־חוּם בַּכְּשָׂבִים וַיִּתֵּן בְּיַד־בָּנָיו: **לו** וַיָּשֶׂם דֶּרֶךְ שְׁלֹשֶׁת יָמִים בֵּינוֹ וּבֵין יַעֲקֹב וְיַעֲקֹב רֹעֶה אֶת־צֹאן לָבָן הַנּוֹתָרֹת:

31) And he said. "What shall I give you?" And Yaakov said, "'Don't give me anything, if you will just do this thing: I will continue to shepherd and watch your shee, p. 32) I will pass through all your sheep today; remove from them all speckled or spotted sheep and all brown sheep among the flock; and the spotted and speckled in the goats, and it will be my wages. 33) And my righteousness will answer for me on the morrow when you come regarding my wages; any which are not spotted or speckled among the goats or brown among the sheep is stolen if it is with me." 34) And Lavan said: "Yes, let it be as you said." 35) *And he removed on that day* the ringed, spotted male goats and all the speckled and spotted female goats, all which had white in them, and all the brown among the sheep and he gave them to his sons. 36) And he put a distance of three days between himself and Yaakov; and Yaakov tended Lavan's remaining sheep.

RASHI, BEREISHIT 30:35

ויסר: לבן ביום ההוא וגו'.

And he removed: Lavan, **on that day**, etc.

This is typical of what I call a Type II comment. Here Rashi adds just one word – "Lavan" – and places it between the Torah's words (bolded above). His intent is clear: he wants to tell us that it was

Lavan, and not Yaakov, who passed through the sheep on that day and removed the spotted he-goats from the flock. It is necessary to tell us this because from the Torah's words – "he removed on that day" – it is not clear who acted, Yaakov or Lavan.

Actually without Rashi's clarification, I would have thought it was Yaakov who passed through, because just a few sentences previously Yaakov says, "I will pass through all your flock today" (verse 32).

Moving to our third level of understanding, we ask: How did Rashi determine that it was Lavan and not Yaakov? The next verse (36) clarifies this. Verse 36 reads: "And he put a distance of three days between himself and Yaakov," etc. Since the subject of this verse is Lavan, the subject of the previous verse must also be Lavan.

For this kind of comment we do not ask "What is bothering Rashi?" because there is no real difficulty in the verse. The more appropriate question is: "What misunderstanding is Rashi helping us avoid?"

Below are some other examples of Type II comments. The first example concerns a war between four kings and five kings in Bereishit:

BEREISHIT 14:4–5

שְׁתֵּים עֶשְׂרֵה שָׁנָה עָבְדוּ אֶת־כְּדָרְלָעֹמֶר וּשְׁלֹשׁ־עֶשְׂרֵה שָׁנָה מָרָדוּ: **וּבְאַרְבַּע עֶשְׂרֵה שָׁנָה** בָּא כְדָרְלָעֹמֶר וְהַמְּלָכִים אֲשֶׁר אִתּוֹ וַיַּכּוּ אֶת־רְפָאִים בְּעַשְׁתְּרֹת קַרְנַיִם וְאֶת־הַזּוּזִים בְּהָם וְאֵת הָאֵימִים בְּשָׁוֵה קִרְיָתָיִם:

Twelve years [the five kings] served Chedorlaomer, and they rebelled thirteen years. *And in the fourteenth year* Chedorlaomer and the kings who were with him came and they struck the Rephaim at Ashteroth-karnaim and the Zuzim in Ham, the Eimim at Shaveh-kiriathaim.

RASHI, BEREISHIT 14:5

ובארבע עשרה שנה: למרדן, **בא כדרלעומר**. לפי שהוא היה בעל המעשה נכנס בעובי הקורה.

And in the fourteenth year: of their rebellion, **Chedorlaomer came.** Since the matter concerned him, "he got into the thick of the matter."

Here Rashi adds the words "of their rebellion" in between the Torah's words. He did this because there is some possibility of confusion. The words ושלש עשרה שנה מרדו may mean that they rebelled "for [an additional] thirteen years," or alternatively "in the thirteenth year." If the latter, the "fourteenth year" would be the fourteenth year counting from the beginning of their servitude, i.e., the second year of their rebellion. Rashi tells us that this is not so. Rather, Chedarlaomer came in the fourteenth year of their rebellion, i.e., twenty-six years after their servitude began. Rashi's brief inserted comment thus comes to correct a possible misunderstanding.

The following example illustrates how Rashi can insert a one-word comment in the middle of a Torah word.

VAYIKRA 10:19

וַיְדַבֵּר אַהֲרֹן אֶל־מֹשֶׁה הֵן הַיּוֹם הִקְרִיבוּ אֶת־חַטָּאתָם וְאֶת־עֹלָתָם לִפְנֵי ה' וַתִּקְרֶאנָה אֹתִי כָּאֵלֶּה **וְאָכַלְתִּי חַטָּאת הַיּוֹם הַיִּיטַב בְּעֵינֵי** ה':

And Aharon spoke to Moshe: "Behold today they have offered their sin offering and their burnt offering before Hashem and these things happened to me. *And [if] I ate a sin offering today, would that have been right* in the eyes of Hashem?"

RASHI

ואכלתי חטאת: ואם אכלתי הייטב וגו'.

And I ate a sin offering: And if I would have eaten, **would that be right**, etc.

Rashi adds the word "if" and inserts it within the Hebrew word *v'achalti*, "and I ate." His purpose was to clarify that Aharon had not actually eaten of the sin offering; he was asking Moshe whether it would have been right *if* he were to have eaten it.

This type of comment is easily recognizable; Rashi simply inserts a word or two between the Torah's words – that is, between the *dibbur hamatchil* and some other words in the verse. The printed *chumashim* always print the *dibbur hamatchil* in bold type, but unfortunately most *chumashim* do not also bold the next words of the verse, so we have to be alert to notice what Rashi is doing.

Keeping these two types of comments in mind will enable the student to find deeper meaning in Rashi's commentary. In chapter 8 we will make some surprising discoveries based on recognizing and understanding this second type of comment.

Chapter 4

Why Does Rashi Translate Familiar Words?

Rashi's magic in commentary can be seen in many ways. This chapter will focus on one of them: Rashi's translation of familiar, easy words. This is a little-discussed aspect of Rashi's commentary which shows how sensitive he was to subtleties in the Torah's language. It also reflects the uniqueness of Rashi's commentary. None of the other classic Torah commentaries had a systematic approach to dealing with simple words that nevertheless need commentary. Rashi was sensitive to such words and commented on them regularly. We will select five examples of Rashi translating simple and familiar words in his commentary. Given that these words appeared many times previously in the Torah – sometimes even just one or two verses previously – Rashi's choice of when to comment was deliberate. Of the examples brought below only one of them was discussed by the famous commentaries on Rashi. In other words, among the tens of thousands who studied Rashi only very few took note of this phenomenon.

We will question why Rashi decided to translate a familiar word on the particular verse that he did, but not when the word was mentioned previously, and we will see how he went about it. We will see that his choice was not an arbitrary one and his reasoning can become apparent to us once we exert the effort to analyze his words closely. Analyzing his approach here will enable us to begin to appreciate Rashi's sensitivity to every word in the Torah. His perceptive eye never rested.

1. Sending the Dove

The following verses are found in parashat Noach. They refer to Noach sending out birds to check if the floodwaters had abated and if there was dry land above the waters.

BEREISHIT 8:7–8

ז וַיְשַׁלַּח אֶת־הָעֹרֵב וַיֵּצֵא יָצוֹא וָשׁוֹב עַד־יְבֹשֶׁת הַמַּיִם מֵעַל הָאָרֶץ:
ח וַיְשַׁלַּח אֶת־הַיּוֹנָה מֵאִתּוֹ לִרְאוֹת הֲקַלּוּ הַמַּיִם מֵעַל פְּנֵי הָאֲדָמָה:

7) *And he sent* the raven; and it went back and forth until the waters dried up from upon the land.

8) *And he sent* the dove from him to see if the waters had abated from upon the earth.

Notice Rashi's comment on the word וישלח in verse 8:

RASHI

וישלח: אין זה לשון שליחות אלא לשון שלוח, שלחה ללכת לדרכה, ובזו יראה אם קלו המים שאם תמצא מנוח לא תשוב אליו.

And he sent: This does not mean "to send [on a mission]" but rather "to set free"; he freed it [the bird] to go its own way and in this way he would see if the waters had subsided, because if she found a place to rest she would not return to him [Noach].

What is Rashi saying?

Rashi tells us that the word וישלח does not mean to send on a mission, as one would send a messenger. Rather here it means to "set free," as Moshe said to Pharaoh: שלח את עמי, "Let my people go free."

The obvious question to ask is: The very same word וישלח appears in the previous verse. Why didn't Rashi tell us its meaning there? Why did he wait until this verse? This is so striking that it is hard to overlook, unless you think that Rashi is not that precise in his commentary.

There is a difference between verses 7 and 8. While verse 7 states that Noach sent out the raven, it doesn't tell us why. Only in verse 8 are we told the purpose for Noach's sending out the dove: "*to see* if the waters had abated from upon the earth."

The addition of these words creates a problem. Who was to see if the waters had abated – Noach or the dove? It couldn't be Noach – he couldn't see; that's why he sent the dove. But it couldn't be the dove either for how was the dove to know what it was to determine? The dove couldn't possibly know the reason that Noach sent him.

This is why Rashi comments on this verse and not on the previous verse. His simple statement answers our question. The dove was not sent on a mission, but instead was set free. Noach knew that the dove would look for a place to land on dry land, and if it found a place it wouldn't return to Noach. In this way Noach would *understand* that there was dry land somewhere. It was Noach who would "see," but "see" here refers to mental seeing, or understanding, as we say in English, "Oh, I see," – meaning "I understand."

We now see (!) why Rashi only commented on this verse and not on the previous one, even though the very same word appears there too. We also see how he explains what had puzzled us – namely, who did the seeing?

This is a striking example of Rashi's sensitivity to detail, which we would have passed over without noticing. Neither the Ramban nor the Ibn Ezra nor the Rashbam – all pursuers of *pshat* – dealt with this problem.

Let us look at some other examples of this sensitivity.

II. Our "Rock"

At the end of the Torah, in the *Ha'azinu* poem, we find another example of Rashi passing over a familiar word several times in quick succession, to finally explain it at a crucial juncture.

DEVARIM 32:31

כִּי לֹא כְצוּרֵנוּ צוּרָם וְאֹיְבֵינוּ פְּלִילִים:

For our rock is not like their rock, and our enemies judge us.

RASHI

כי לא כצורנו צורם: כל זה היה להם לאויבים להבין שהשם הסגירם ולא להם ולאלוהיהם הניצחון, שהרי עד הנה לא יכלו כלום אלוהיהם כנגד צורנו, כי לא כסלענו סלעם. **כל צור שבמקרא לשון סלע.**

For our rock is not like their rock: All this the enemies should have understood: that Hashem gave [Israel] over to them and victory was not due to them or their gods. For until now their gods had not been able to do anything against our rock. For our rock [סלע] is not like their rock [סלע]. *Every time the word* צור *appears in the Torah it means "rock."*

In his last words Rashi is telling us that the word צור means סלע, which means "rock." But the word צור has already appeared several times in this chapter before this verse! Examples of this are:

ד הַצּוּר תָּמִים פָּעֳלוֹ

4) The *tzur* – His work is perfect

יג וַיֵּנִקֵהוּ דְבַשׁ מִסֶּלַע וְשֶׁמֶן מֵחַלְמִישׁ **צוּר**

13) And He would suckle him with honey from a rock, and oil from a flinty *tzur*

טו וַיְנַבֵּל **צוּר** יְשֻׁעָתוֹ

15) And he was contemptuous of the *tzur* of his salvation

יח **צוּר** יְלָדְךָ תֶּשִׁי

18) You ignored the *tzur* who gave birth to you

ל אִם־לֹא כִּי־**צוּרָם** מְכָרָם

30) If not that their *tzur* sold them out

Then comes our verse:

כִּי לֹא כְצוּרֵנוּ **צוּרָם** וְאֹיְבֵינוּ פְּלִילִים

For our *tzur* is not like their *tzur*, and our enemies judge us

Why did Rashi wait until this verse to comment? He had five other mentions of the word צור previously but did not comment on them.

A form of the word צור appears in a familiar verse in Yeshayahu 45:7:

יוֹצֵר אוֹר וּבוֹרֵא חֹשֶׁךְ עֹשֶׂה שָׁלוֹם וּבוֹרֵא רָע אֲנִי ה' עֹשֶׂה כָל אֵלֶּה׃

He *formed* light and created darkness; He makes peace and created evil. I am Hashem Who made all these.

We see from the above quotes that the word צור can have two possible meanings. It can mean "Creator," as in the verse from Yeshayahu. Or it can mean "rock," as Rashi says here.

In all the previous verses the word צור referred to Hashem. Therefore, in these verses both meanings of the word are correct. Rashi made no comment to clarify which meaning was true, since both meanings are appropriate in reference to Hashem.

But in our verse the word refers both to the Jewish G-d and to the enemy's pagan god. It was at this point – and only at this point – that Rashi had to clarify its meaning, lest the student think that צור meant "Creator" even when referring to the pagan god. That is why here and only here does Rashi need to tell us that צור only means rock.

III. You Were Strangers

The following comes from parashat Mishpatim, where the Torah teaches us sensitivity and correct conduct to the stranger.

SHEMOT 22:20

וְגֵר לֹא־תוֹנֶה וְלֹא תִלְחָצֶנּוּ כִּי־גֵרִים הֱיִיתֶם בְּאֶרֶץ מִצְרָיִם:

You shall not taunt or oppress a stranger *for you were strangers* in the land of Egypt.

RASHI

כי גרים הייתם: אם הוניתו, אף הוא יכול להונותך ולומר לך אף אתה מגרים באת, מום שבך אל תאמר לחברך. כל לשון גר, אדם שלא נולד באותה מדינה, אלא בא ממדינה אחרת לגור שם.

For you were strangers: If you verbally abuse him, he too can abuse you, saying, "You too came from strangers!" Do not accuse a person of a flaw that you yourself have. *Any use of the word* גר *(stranger) in the Torah means a person who was not born in that country but came from another country to live there.*

The question again is: Why did Rashi wait until this verse to comment?

The word גר appears in the Torah many times before this. Below are some examples:

BEREISHIT 15:13

וַיֹּאמֶר לְאַבְרָם יָדֹעַ תֵּדַע כִּי־גֵר יִהְיֶה זַרְעֲךָ בְּאֶרֶץ לֹא לָהֶם וַעֲבָדוּם וְעִנּוּ אֹתָם אַרְבַּע מֵאוֹת שָׁנָה:

And He said to Avram: "You should certainly know that your children will be *strangers* in a land not theirs, and they will serve them; and they will oppress them four hundred years."

SHEMOT 2:22

וַתֵּלֶד בֵּן וַיִּקְרָא אֶת שְׁמוֹ גֵּרְשֹׁם כִּי אָמַר גֵּר הָיִיתִי בְּאֶרֶץ נָכְרִיָּה:

And she bore a son and he called his name Gershom for he said, "I have been a *stranger* in a strange land."

SHEMOT 12:48

וְכִי יָגוּר אִתְּךָ גֵּר וְעָשָׂה פֶסַח לַה' הִמּוֹל לוֹ כָל זָכָר וְאָז יִקְרַב לַעֲשֹׂתוֹ וְהָיָה כְּאֶזְרַח הָאָרֶץ וְכָל עָרֵל לֹא יֹאכַל בּוֹ:

And when a *stranger* dwells with you and he will make the Pesach offering to Hashem, he must circumcise every male and then he can come near to offer it and he will be like every native of the land, but no uncircumcised shall eat of it.

Why did Rashi wait until our verse to comment when he had at least three previous verses to explain the meaning of the word גר?

The word גר (stranger) in our verse is understood by the rabbis to refer to a convert. The mitzva learned from this verse is not to insult or otherwise abuse a convert. But if we translate גר in this verse as "convert," the reasoning of "because you were converts in Egypt" does not make sense. We were not converts in Egypt! We were strangers to the Egyptians, but we were not converts. We were all sons of Avraham, Yitzchak and Yaakov, so how can the verse make such a comparison?

That is what Rashi is dealing with in his comment.

Rashi's comment is based on a Talmudic source in tractate *Baba Metzia* (59b). There it says: "Why does the Torah say, 'And do not abuse or pressure a *ger* [convert]'? Rav Natan said: 'A flaw that you have, do not accuse another of it.'" Rashi on the Talmud there notes: "Since you were גרים it is an insult to mention the word גר." What Rashi means is that just the sound of the word גר, no matter what type of גר – convert or immigrant – is chilling to the גר who hears the comment. Therefore do not say this word to a convert.

That is why Rashi has to clarify here that in truth the word גר means an immigrant (as if to say, I know the Jews were not converts as the subject of our verse is), nevertheless don't ever use this word in the presence of a convert – when he hears it, it is upsetting to him.

IV. Wandering after Our Hearts

Below is yet another example of Rashi's craft. Through understanding Rashi's precision in choosing the particular word for comparison, we will learn a moral lesson as well.

This example refers to the mitzva of tzitzit, which is found at the end of parashat Shelach and comes directly after the story of the spies whom Moshe sent to check out the land of Canaan.

BAMIDBAR 15:39

וְהָיָה לָכֶם לְצִיצִת וּרְאִיתֶם אֹתוֹ וּזְכַרְתֶּם אֶת כָּל מִצְוֹת ה' וַעֲשִׂיתֶם אֹתָם **וְלֹא תָתוּרוּ אַחֲרֵי לְבַבְכֶם** וְאַחֲרֵי עֵינֵיכֶם אֲשֶׁר אַתֶּם זֹנִים אַחֲרֵיהֶם:

And it shall be for you tzitzit and you shall see it and remember all the mitzvot of Hashem and you shall do them *and you shall not wander after your heart* and after your eyes, after which you go astray.

RASHI

ולא תתורו אחרי לבבכם: כמו "מתור הארץ" (יג:כה). הלב
והעינים הם מרגלים לגוף ומסרסרים לו את העבירות: העין
רואה והלב חומד והגוף עושה את העבירות.

And you shall not wander after your heart: [The word תתורו] is similar to the word מתור הארץ, "from spying out the land" (above 13:25). The heart and the eyes are the spies for the body, procuring sins for it: the eye sees, the heart desires and the body commits the sin.

There are two parts to this Rashi comment. The first part tells us the derivation and meaning of the word תתורו ("you shall spy out"). Rashi refers back to the word's previous mention in our parasha, when the spies came back from "spying [מתור] the land." The second part of this comment imparts a psychological lesson and moral warning about how we may be seduced into sinning.

In this comment we again find the same phenomenon: In the story of the spies the root תור (to spy) is used no less than a *dozen* times. Of this list of twelve times, Rashi chooses one of the middle times that this word is used. Why didn't Rashi comment the first time this word appeared in the parasha?

In addition, Rashi will frequently compare a word in one verse to the same word elsewhere in the Torah or in the Tanach in order to understand its meaning. It is reasonable for him to find the closest place the word appears. Hence we must always wonder when Rashi chooses the comparison word from a distant reference when a closer one exists.

So we ask: Of all the times this word appears in this parasha, why did Rashi choose this one in particular to use as his source? It was neither the closest example nor was it the first one in our section.

The word Rashi noted is found in verse 13:25: "They returned from spying out the land at the end of forty days." It was precisely at this point that their mission turned sour. It was at this point that we begin to see that their spying out the land was for negative motives. Soon after this verse they begin their disparaging report about the land.

The word "to search" or "to spy" can have either a positive or a negative connotation. Moshe sent the spies on a positive mission; they were the ones who turned it into a negative and ultimately self-destructive experience. It would seem that Rashi's search for a similar word was not just philological. He was not only interested in letting us know the derivation of the word תתורו, he also wanted to find the moral equivalent to the meaning of the word in our chapter about tzitzit. Our verse says in effect: Don't follow the negative impulses of your heart. To serve his purpose, Rashi thus chose the first time that the word תור had a negative connotation in the story of the spies.

v. Doors and Openings

The following is an excellent and cogent example of Rashi's approach. I suggest we use it as a learning experience. I will present the question, without the answer. Try to answer it yourself. An answer is found in the appendix.

BEREISHIT 19:6–11

ו וַיֵּצֵא אֲלֵהֶם לוֹט **הַפֶּתְחָה וְהַדֶּלֶת** סָגַר אַחֲרָיו: ז וַיֹּאמַר אַל־נָא אַחַי תָּרֵעוּ: ח הִנֵּה־נָא לִי שְׁתֵּי בָנוֹת אֲשֶׁר לֹא־יָדְעוּ אִישׁ אוֹצִיאָה־נָּא אֶתְהֶן אֲלֵיכֶם וַעֲשׂוּ לָהֶן כַּטּוֹב בְּעֵינֵיכֶם רַק לָאֲנָשִׁים הָאֵל אַל־תַּעֲשׂוּ דָבָר כִּי־עַל־כֵּן בָּאוּ בְּצֵל קֹרָתִי: ט וַיֹּאמְרוּ גֶּשׁ־הָלְאָה וַיֹּאמְרוּ הָאֶחָד בָּא־לָגוּר וַיִּשְׁפֹּט שָׁפוֹט עַתָּה נָרַע לְךָ מֵהֶם וַיִּפְצְרוּ בָאִישׁ בְּלוֹט מְאֹד וַיִּגְּשׁוּ לִשְׁבֹּר **הַדָּלֶת**: י וַיִּשְׁלְחוּ הָאֲנָשִׁים אֶת־יָדָם וַיָּבִיאוּ אֶת־לוֹט אֲלֵיהֶם הַבָּיְתָה וְאֶת־**הַדֶּלֶת** סָגָרוּ: יא וְאֶת־הָאֲנָשִׁים אֲשֶׁר־**פֶּתַח** הַבַּיִת הִכּוּ בַּסַּנְוֵרִים מִקָּטֹן וְעַד־גָּדוֹל וַיִּלְאוּ לִמְצֹא הַ**פָּתַח**:

6) And Lot went out to them towards the *opening*; and the *door* was closed after him. 7) And he said: "Please, my brothers, do no harm. 8) Here are my two daughters, who have known no men. I will bring them out to you; do with them as is good in your eyes; only do nothing to these men because they have come to the shelter of my house." 9) And they said, "Go over there"; and they said, "One comes to dwell and he now has become a judge – now you are worse than them." And they pressed the man, Lot, very much, and they drew near to break the *door*. 10) And the men stretched out their hand and brought Lot to them into the house, and they closed the *door*. 11) And the men who were in the *opening* of the house were struck with blindness from the young until the old and they struggled to find the *opening*.

RASHI

(ט) **הדלת**: דלת הסובבת לנעול ולפתוח.
(יא) **פתח**: הוא החלל שבו נכנסין ויוצאין.

(9) **The door**: *Delet*, which swivels to lock and to open.

(11) **Opening**: The hollow space in which one enters and exits.

The question that begs to be asked is: Does Rashi really need to tell us what a דלת (door) is, or what a פתח (opening) is? A five-year-old child knows the meaning of these words. And if for any reason Rashi does have to tell us their meaning, then why didn't he comment on these same two words in verse 6?!

None of the classic Rashi commentators says anything here. Yet we must ask this, because understanding *what* Rashi says is simply not enough when *why* he says it is not at all obvious.

When we think about this example we realize that we could

have read these verses hundreds of times without understanding what Rashi did. Here again is an example of Rashi's exquisitely perceptive eye.

What is your answer? (See the appendix, page 130.)

Chapter 5

Rashi's Use of Midrash

It is estimated that about 70 percent of Rashi's comments on the Torah are from the Midrash or the Talmud; most of these are not obviously *pshat* interpretations. As we study Rashi's comments we will see that there is always a reasonable explanation for his choosing the midrash that he does. We also see that Rashi is not a passive "collector of midrashim." He doesn't just "cut and paste" midrashim from the wide collection that exists and insert them into his commentary. Rashi consciously selects midrashim and subtly rewords them in order to suit the purposes of his commentary – i.e., to answer difficulties in the text. Rashi's careful use of Midrash reveals his masterful craftsmanship.

We will examine and illustrate some of the different ways Rashi relates to and changes the midrash that he uses in his commentary. These include:

1. Selecting one midrash from among many
2. Rejecting a midrash
3. Changing the location of a midrash
4. Changing the wording of a midrash
5. Combining words of two separate midrashim
6. Creating his own midrash

1. Rashi Selects One Midrash from Among Many

The following is an illustrative example of Rashi's technique of choosing one of several midrashim.

BEREISHIT 27:1

וַיְהִי כִּי־זָקֵן יִצְחָק **וַתִּכְהֶיןָ** עֵינָיו מֵרְאֹת וַיִּקְרָא אֶת־עֵשָׂו...

And it was when Yitzchak became old and his eyes *were dimmed* from seeing and he called to Esav....

RASHI

ותכהין: בעשנן של אלו שהיו מעשנות ומקטירות לעבודה זרה. דבר אחר: כדי שיטול יעקב את הברכות.

[**His eyes**] **were dimmed:** Because of the smoke of these [women] who would burn incense for idol worship.

Another explanation: To enable Yaakov to receive the blessings.

Rashi chose two explanations for Yitzchak's blindness, which derive from the Midrash. The second can easily be seen as *pshat*, even though its source is the Midrash. But what is relevant for us is that there are at least three other midrashic explanations of this verse which Rashi did *not* choose.

"When Yitzchak was bound on the altar for slaughter...the ministering angels cried and their tears fell upon his eyes and as a result his eyesight dimmed." (*Bereishit Rabba* 66:9)

"Rav Eliezer said: The eyes of one who looks at an evil person will become dimmed as it says, 'And it was when Yitzchak grew old and his eyes became dim from seeing...' – because he looked at the evil Esav, this is what caused it." (*Megilla* 28a)

"Rav Yitzchak said: One should never make light of an ordinary person's curse. Avimelech cursed Sarah, and the curse was fulfilled in her offspring [Yitzchak], as it says, 'Behold, this is for you for a covering of the eyes' (Bereishit 26:16)." (*Megilla*, ibid.)

Rashi was aware of these midrashim; nevertheless he chose not to use them for his commentary on this verse. Why? And why did he choose the ones he did use?

Rashi had said in his comment in Bereishit 3:8 that his goal in commentary was to quote *"aggada* that serves to clarify the words of Scripture." The two midrashim that Rashi chose have a reasonable connection to the context within which this verse finds itself. The first midrash refers to Esav's wives; the previous verse had stated that they caused Yitzchak and Rivka bitterness. The second midrash shows how Yitzchak's blindness is a lead-in to the story that follows, about the stealing of the blessings. Yaakov was only able to steal the blessings because Yitzchak was blind and couldn't distinguish between the two brothers.

The midrashim that were *not* used by Rashi, on the other hand, have nothing to do with either the context of the verse or its wording. This is what Rashi meant when he stated that he would use *aggada* to clarify Scripture's words. It is important to remember this. When Rashi includes a particular midrash in his commentary, he chooses and selects from among several midrashim. With this rule in mind, we can better understand why he chose a particular midrash *and* what its relevance is to the verse.

11. Rashi Rejects a Midrash

A superficial reading of Rashi's commentary, in which he includes many midrashim, would lead one to think that Rashi chose midrashim at random. Yet in truth Rashi rejected midrashim that did not conform to his standard.

Below are some examples of Rashi rejecting midrashim – sometimes he does this explicitly, sometimes he just hints at the existence of midrashim without citing them, and sometimes he will mention *pshat* without even hinting at the existence of a midrash. Understanding Rashi's approach to midrashim enables us to appreciate some Rashi comments that have puzzled commentaries for centuries.

SHEMOT 33:13

וְעַתָּה אִם־נָא מָצָאתִי חֵן בְּעֵינֶיךָ הוֹדִעֵנִי נָא אֶת־דְּרָכֶךָ וְאֵדָעֲךָ לְמַעַן אֶמְצָא־חֵן בְּעֵינֶיךָ וּרְאֵה כִּי עַמְּךָ הַגּוֹי הַזֶּה:

And now, if I have found favor in Your eyes, please let me know Your ways, so I will know You in order that I shall find favor in Your eyes; *and see that they are Your people, this nation.*

RASHI

וראה כי עמך הגוי הזה: שלא תאמר "ואעשה אותך לגוי גדול", ואת אלה תעזוב. ראה כי עמך הם מקדם, ואם בהם תמאס, איני סומך על היוצאים מחלצי שיתקיימו, ואת תשלום השכר שלי בעם הזה תודיעני. ורבותינו דרשוהו במסכת ברכות (דף ז א). **ואני ליישב המקראות על אופניהם ועל סדרם באתי.**

And they are Your people, this nation: You should not say "And I will make *you* a great nation" and abandon these. Rather, "See they are Your people from previously" and if You despise them I don't rely on my descendents to survive; but if you will pay me my reward through this nation, let me know. *The rabbis had a midrash on this* (in Berachot 7a). *But I [come to] explain Scripture in their proper setting and order.*

Rashi's last words are very important. They tell us that he disagrees with the Midrash interpretation because it does not accord with his requirements for his Torah commentary.

Let us examine the midrash that Rashi rejects:

> [Moshe] asked to be shown the ways of the Holy One, blessed be He, and it was granted to him. For it is said, "Show me now Your ways." Moshe said before Him, "Lord of the Universe, why is it that some righteous men prosper and others are in adversity, some wicked men prosper and others are in adversity?"

We now can see why Rashi rejects this midrash as a possible *drash* interpretation of this verse. The age-old theological question of "Why do bad things happen to good people?" would certainly be answered if Hashem "revealed His ways" to Moshe. But as Rashi himself points out, he is interested in his commentary to "explain the words of Scripture in *their proper setting and order*." The philosophical question that the midrash puts into Moshe's mouth has nothing to do with the context of these verses, so Rashi rejected the midrash.

Another example will add to our understanding. This next example is taken from the story of Lot and the destruction of Sodom.

BEREISHIT 19:15

וּכְמוֹ הַשַּׁחַר עָלָה וַיָּאִיצוּ הַמַּלְאָכִים בְּלוֹט לֵאמֹר קוּם קַח אֶת־אִשְׁתְּךָ וְאֶת־שְׁתֵּי בְנֹתֶיךָ הַנִּמְצָאֹת פֶּן־תִּסָּפֶה בַּעֲוֹן הָעִיר:

And as the dawn began the messengers urged Lot saying, "Rise, take your wife and your two daughters *who are here*, lest you perish because of the sin of the city."

RASHI

הנמצאות: המזומנות לך בבית להצילם. ומדרש אגדה יש, וזה יישובו של מקרא.

Who are here: Who are available to you in the house for you to save them. And there are *midrashei aggada*, but this fits best with the [words of] Scripture.

This is a perfect example of Rashi giving us simple *pshat* and then explicitly saying that the midrashim on this verse are not compatible with the text.

Which midrash is Rashi rejecting?

BEREISHIT RABBA 50:10

אמר רבי טוביה בר רבי יצחק: שתי מציאות – רות המואביה ונעמה העמונית.

Rav Tuvia son of Rav Yitzchak said: Two *"metziot"* [valuable findings] – Rut the Moabite and Naama the Ammonite.

This is a typical midrash – it transcends time and place! Rut and Naama lived hundreds of years after Lot and in different countries. The reason these two women are chosen is because in the next chapter Lot impregnates his two daughters, who then give birth to Moav and Ammon, the forefathers of Rut and Naama. Rashi rejects the midrash because it is certainly not *pshat*, since it does not fit into the context of the verse. For other examples of Rashi explicitly rejecting a midrash see Bereishit 3:22, 20:16; Shemot 6:9, 23:2; and Vayikra 13:55.

We can now understand another Rashi comment that has puzzled commentators. In the following verses Yaakov is blessing his son Yoseph and his grandchildren.

BEREISHIT 48:8–20

וַיַּרְא יִשְׂרָאֵל אֶת־בְּנֵי יוֹסֵף וַיֹּאמֶר מִי־אֵלֶּה: וַיֹּאמֶר יוֹסֵף אֶל־אָבִיו בָּנַי הֵם אֲשֶׁר־נָתַן־לִי אֱלֹקִים בָּזֶה וַיֹּאמַר קָחֶם־נָא אֵלַי וַאֲבָרֲכֵם: וְעֵינֵי יִשְׂרָאֵל כָּבְדוּ מִזֹּקֶן לֹא יוּכַל לִרְאוֹת וַיַּגֵּשׁ אֹתָם אֵלָיו וַיִּשַּׁק לָהֶם וַיְחַבֵּק לָהֶם: וַיֹּאמֶר יִשְׂרָאֵל אֶל־יוֹסֵף רְאֹה פָנֶיךָ לֹא פִלָּלְתִּי וְהִנֵּה הֶרְאָה אֹתִי אֱלֹקִים גַּם אֶת־זַרְעֶךָ: וַיּוֹצֵא יוֹסֵף אֹתָם מֵעִם בִּרְכָּיו וַיִּשְׁתַּחוּ לְאַפָּיו אָרְצָה: וַיִּקַּח יוֹסֵף אֶת־שְׁנֵיהֶם אֶת־**אֶפְרַיִם** בִּימִינוֹ מִשְּׂמֹאל יִשְׂרָאֵל וְאֶת־**מְנַשֶּׁה** בִשְׂמֹאלוֹ מִימִין יִשְׂרָאֵל וַיַּגֵּשׁ אֵלָיו: וַיִּשְׁלַח יִשְׂרָאֵל אֶת־יְמִינוֹ וַיָּשֶׁת עַל־רֹאשׁ אֶפְרַיִם וְהוּא הַצָּעִיר וְאֶת־שְׂמֹאלוֹ עַל־רֹאשׁ מְנַשֶּׁה שִׂכֵּל אֶת־יָדָיו כִּי מְנַשֶּׁה הַבְּכוֹר: וַיְבָרֶךְ אֶת־יוֹסֵף וַיֹּאמַר הָאֱלֹקִים אֲשֶׁר הִתְהַלְּכוּ אֲבֹתַי לְפָנָיו אַבְרָהָם וְיִצְחָק הָאֱלֹקִים הָרֹעֶה אֹתִי מֵעוֹדִי עַד־הַיּוֹם הַזֶּה: הַמַּלְאָךְ הַגֹּאֵל אֹתִי מִכָּל־רָע **יְבָרֵךְ** אֶת־**הַנְּעָרִים** וְיִקָּרֵא בָהֶם שְׁמִי וְשֵׁם אֲבֹתַי אַבְרָהָם וְיִצְחָק וְיִדְגּוּ לָרֹב בְּקֶרֶב הָאָרֶץ: וַיַּרְא יוֹסֵף כִּי־יָשִׁית אָבִיו יַד־יְמִינוֹ עַל־רֹאשׁ אֶפְרַיִם וַיֵּרַע בְּעֵינָיו וַיִּתְמֹךְ יַד־אָבִיו לְהָסִיר אֹתָהּ מֵעַל רֹאשׁ־אֶפְרַיִם עַל־רֹאשׁ מְנַשֶּׁה: וַיֹּאמֶר יוֹסֵף אֶל־

RASHI'S USE OF MIDRASH

אָבִיו לֹא־כֵן אָבִי כִּי־זֶה הַבְּכֹר שִׂים יְמִינְךָ עַל־רֹאשׁוֹ: וַיְמָאֵן אָבִיו וַיֹּאמֶר יָדַעְתִּי בְנִי יָדַעְתִּי גַּם־הוּא יִהְיֶה־לְעָם וְגַם־הוּא יִגְדַּל וְאוּלָם אָחִיו הַקָּטֹן יִגְדַּל מִמֶּנּוּ וְזַרְעוֹ יִהְיֶה מְלֹא־הַגּוֹיִם: **וַיְבָרֲכֵם בַּיּוֹם הַהוּא לֵאמוֹר** בְּךָ יְבָרֵךְ יִשְׂרָאֵל לֵאמֹר יְשִׂמְךָ אֱלֹקִים כְּאֶפְרַיִם וְכִמְנַשֶּׁה וַיָּשֶׂם אֶת־אֶפְרַיִם לִפְנֵי מְנַשֶּׁה:

And Israel saw the sons of Yoseph and said, "Who are they?" And Yoseph said to his father, "They are my sons, which G-d has given me." And [Yaakov] said, "Bring them to me and I will bless them." ... And he brought them near to him.... And he blessed Yoseph saying: "The G-d before Whom my fathers – Avraham and Yitzchak – walked, the G-d Who shepherds me from my beginning until this day. May the angel who redeems me from all evil, *bless the lads* and call them by my name and the name of my fathers, Avraham and Yitzchak, and they should proliferate greatly in the land."

I have quoted all these verses in Hebrew, and translated most of them, so you can review them as we analyze Rashi's comment.

RASHI, BEREISHIT 48:16

יברך את הנערים: מנשה ואפרים.

He shall bless the lads: Menashe and Ephraim.

This comment has puzzled all Rashi commentators, because it is obvious that "the lads" refers to Menashe and Ephraim. Since the whole section speaks only of Menashe and Ephraim, it is clear that "the lads" refers to them. Why does Rashi need to tell us what is self-understood?

The commentaries on Rashi make various attempts to explain this curiosity. Mizrachi, the most famous commentator on Rashi, writes:

It was necessary to explain this even though it is self-understood, because a later verse says "And he blessed them on that day" (20), which implies that at this point he had not yet blessed them. I might therefore have thought that the lads mentioned here are younger sons of Yoseph *who were not fit to bring because of their young age.*

This answer is problematic for several reasons. First of all, we have heard nothing about Yoseph having any other children, so why should we now assume he has any? And secondly, the Mizrachi contradicts himself in explaining a Rashi comment a few verses previously.

Verse 6 reads:

וּמוֹלַדְתְּךָ אֲשֶׁר־הוֹלַדְתָּ אַחֲרֵיהֶם לְךָ יִהְיוּ עַל שֵׁם אֲחֵיהֶם יִקָּרְאוּ בְּנַחֲלָתָם:

But your progeny *which you begat* after them shall be yours; they will be included under the name of their brothers with regard to their inheritance.

RASHI

אשר הולדת: אם תוליד עוד.

Which you begat: If you will beget more [children].

MIZRACHI

The word אשר should be understood to mean "if" and the word הוליד, in the past tense, should be read as if it were in the future tense, because if the meaning is as is stated [that he already had other, younger children] then he should have brought them to his father in order to receive the blessing. And *we should not say that he did not bring them because they were too young,* because the blessing of a prophet [Yaakov] is a blessing from G-d and *one should not have them miss this just because they are very young!*

We see that the Mizrachi contradicts himself – in one place he says Yoseph might have brought other, younger children if he had them; while on our verse he says he might not bring the very young children.

An explanation of this apparently redundant Rashi comment can be found in a statement by the *Sefer Zikaron* in parashat Shemot. There he says that there are times when Rashi will make an obvious, apparently unnecessary comment in order to exclude a particular midrashic interpretation.

On the verse about "the lads" there is in fact a very interesting midrash. The midrash says that the words יברך את הנערים refer to Yehoshua and Gidon (*Bereishit Rabba* 97:3). This is strange for both of them lived several years after Yaakov's time.

But there are curious similarities to our verse:

1. Yehoshua was from the tribe of Ephraim and Gidon was from the tribe of Menashe.
2. In our verse Yaakov mentions "the angel who redeems me." Both Yehoshua and Gidon met angels of G-d (Yehoshua 5:13; Shoftim 6:12).
3. The verse refers to the boys as נערים (lads). Yehoshua was called a lad (Shemot 33:11) and Gidon claimed to be the youngest in his family (Shoftim 6:15).

It is likely that all these striking similarities made this non-*pshat* midrash appealing to many. So Rashi came to disabuse us of this mistaken interpretation with his down-to-earth comment – the lads are (just) Ephraim and Menashe.

The purpose of this self-understood Rashi comment, then, is to reject the appealing – but not *pshat* – midrash.

III. Rashi Changes the Location of a Midrash

Another example of Rashi's creative use of Midrash is when he cites a midrash from one verse but applies it to a different verse.

This is not an unusual occurrence in his commentary. It is always a challenge to understand why he makes this transfer.

A clear example of this occurs in Bereishit 24. Eliezer, Avraham's servant, had been sent to find a wife for Yitzchak. As he tells Rivka's family about the conversation he had had with Avraham before he left, he says the following:

BEREISHIT 24:39

וָאֹמַר אֶל־אֲדֹנִי אֻלַי לֹא־תֵלֵךְ הָאִשָּׁה אַחֲרָי...

"And I said to my master, '*Perhaps the woman will not come after me.*'"

RASHI

אלי לא תלך האשה: אלי כתיב. בת היתה לו לאליעזר והיה מחזר למצוא עילה שיאמר לו אברהם לפנות אליו להשיאו בתו. אמר לו אברהם, "בני ברוך ואתה ארור, ואין ארור מדבק בברוך".

Perhaps the woman will not come: It is written אֵלַי [not אוּלַי]. Eliezer had a daughter and was looking for a pretext so that Avraham would tell him that he is turning to him to allow his [Eliezer's] daughter to marry [Yitzchak]. But Avraham said to him, "My son is blessed and you are cursed. One who is cursed cannot cleave to one who is blessed."

Rashi's source is found in *Bereishit Rabba*, but with some differences. Firstly, the midrash is found on an earlier verse (Bereishit 24:5):

וַיֹּאמֶר אֵלָיו הָעֶבֶד **אֻלַי** לֹא־תֹאבֶה הָאִשָּׁה לָלֶכֶת אַחֲרַי אֶל־הָאָרֶץ הַזֹּאת הֶהָשֵׁב אָשִׁיב אֶת־בִּנְךָ אֶל־הָאָרֶץ אֲשֶׁר־יָצָאתָ מִשָּׁם:

And the servant said to him: "*Perhaps* the woman will not want to come after me to this land; shall I return your son to the land that you left?"

Here Eliezer is speaking with Avraham, whereas in our verse Eliezer is retelling that conversation to Rivka's family.

The second difference concerns the basis for the midrash. The midrash is not built on the fact that the word אוּלַי is spelled without a ו, for in the verse that the midrash comments on the word is spelled correctly! Rashi, however, does make a point of the spelling because in the verse that he is commenting on the spelling is strange. Rashi points out that since the word is spelled without a ו, it could be read as אֵלַי, meaning "to me." This, for Rashi, is the basis of the *drash* that Eliezer hoped that Avraham would turn to him. In moving the midrash from 24:5 to 24:39, Rashi has changed the basis for the midrash.

Two questions can be asked regarding Rashi's change of location:

1. Why didn't Rashi comment on the first verse, as the midrash did?

    and

2. Why did he move the midrash to this verse and comment on it?

Rashi certainly made this change intentionally. We can only speculate as to the reason. But it would seem that Rashi wanted the midrash to explain the unusual spelling of the word אלי. This is what was bothering him and the midrash afforded an explanation of this anomaly.

The midrash in *Bereishit Rabba* itself, on the other hand, was not concerned with the strange spelling; it was giving us an interpretation of verse 5. There Eliezer used the word אולי, meaning "perhaps," but this word is used throughout Tanach when one hopes something good will happen, in the sense of "perchance." Since Eliezer was telling Avraham that things may not work out as his master had wanted, it would have been more appropriate to use the word פֶּן, which means "lest" and is appropriate when forecasting an unwanted event. This is the basis for the midrash and therefore it commented at the first opportunity, on verse 24:5.

We see that the goals of Midrash and the goals of Rashi, as a Torah commentator, are not always identical. Here is another example of Rashi changing the location of a midrash:

BEREISHIT 24:52

וַיְהִי כַּאֲשֶׁר שָׁמַע עֶבֶד אַבְרָהָם אֶת־דִּבְרֵיהֶם וַיִּשְׁתַּחוּ אַרְצָה לַה׳:

And it was when the servant of Avraham heard their words; *and he bowed earthward* to Hashem.

RASHI

וישתחו ארצה: מכאן שמודים על בשורה טובה.

And he bowed earthward: From here we learn that one must thank [G-d] upon hearing good news.

Rashi's comment is taken from a midrash, but the midrash was said on verse 26 of this chapter:

וַיִּקֹּד הָאִישׁ וַיִּשְׁתַּחוּ לַה׳:

And the man bowed his head and prostrated himself to Hashem.

The difference between verses 26 and 52 is that the first time Eliezer thanked G-d, his mission had not yet been completed; Eliezer had discovered that Rivka was a relative of Avraham's and he had witnessed her kindness and hospitality, but Rivka's family had not yet consented to the marriage. Only in verse 52 did Eliezer know for certain that G-d had blessed his efforts with success, because the family had agreed that Rivka would be Yitzchak's wife. So here, in verse 52, he thanked G-d for news that was truly good; it is for this reason that Rashi applied the midrash here.

Here again the individual approaches of Midrash and Rashi

manifest themselves. The Midrash uses the verse to convey an idea, or a moral lesson. Rashi, on the other hand, uses the Midrash to clarify the meaning of the verse.

The Midrash could make its moral lesson even on verse 26, because Eliezer was grateful even at this early point in his mission. Rashi, on the other hand, quoted the Midrash only when Eliezer's gratitude was truly justified – once Eliezer knew he had found a wife for Yitzchak.

And yet another example:

BAMIDBAR 22:35

וַיֹּאמֶר מַלְאַךְ ה' אֶל־בִּלְעָם לֵךְ עִם־הָאֲנָשִׁים וְאֶפֶס אֶת־הַדָּבָר אֲשֶׁר־אֲדַבֵּר אֵלֶיךָ אֹתוֹ תְדַבֵּר וַיֵּלֶךְ בִּלְעָם עִם־שָׂרֵי בָלָק:

And the angel of Hashem said to Bilam, "*Go with the men*, but you will only speak that which I speak to you"; and Bilam went with the officers of Balak.

RASHI

לך עם האנשים: בדרך שאדם רוצה לילך בה, מוליכין אותו. "לך עם האנשים", כי חלקך עימהם וסופך להיאבד מן העולם.

Go with the men: The way a person wants to go, that is the way he is taken; "Go with the men" – because your lot is with them and you will ultimately perish from the world.

Rashi's source is a midrash, but this midrash was connected to verse 20, earlier in the chapter:

BAMIDBAR 22:20–22

כ וַיָּבֹא אֱלֹקִים אֶל־בִּלְעָם לַיְלָה וַיֹּאמֶר לוֹ אִם־לִקְרֹא לְךָ בָּאוּ הָאֲנָשִׁים קוּם לֵךְ אִתָּם וְאַךְ אֶת־הַדָּבָר אֲשֶׁר־אֲדַבֵּר אֵלֶיךָ אֹתוֹ תַעֲשֶׂה: **כא** וַיָּקָם בִּלְעָם בַּבֹּקֶר וַיַּחֲבֹשׁ אֶת־אֲתֹנוֹ וַיֵּלֶךְ עִם־שָׂרֵי מוֹאָב: **כב** וַיִּחַר־אַף אֱלֹקִים כִּי־הוֹלֵךְ הוּא וַיִּתְיַצֵּב מַלְאַךְ ה' בַּדֶּרֶךְ לְשָׂטָן לוֹ וְהוּא רֹכֵב עַל־אֲתֹנוֹ וּשְׁנֵי נְעָרָיו עִמּוֹ:

20) And G-d came to Bilam by night and said to him, "*If the men came to call you, get up and go with them*, but only the thing that I shall speak to you, that shall you do." 21) And Bilam arose in the morning and saddled his donkey and went with the officers of Moav. 22) And G-d's wrath flared because he was going and an angel of Hashem stood in the way to impede him. He was riding on his donkey and his two lads were with him.

TANCHUMA 8

אם לקרוא לך באו האנשים קום לך אתם: מכאן אתה למד שבדרך שאדם רוצה לילך, בה מוליכין אותו. שמתחלה נאמר לו (כב:יב), "לא תלך עימהם". כיון שהעיז פניו להלך עימהם, הלך. שכן כתוב בו (כב:כב), "ויחר אף אלהים כי הולך הוא". אמר לו הקדוש ברוך הוא: "איני חפץ באבודן של רשעים. הואיל ואת רוצה ליאבד מן העולם, קום לך אתם."

If the men came to call you, get up and go with them: From here we learn that the way a person wants to go, that is the way he is taken. For at first he was told "Do not go with them" (22:12), but since he brazenly went with them, as it says "And G-d was angry that he went" (22:22), so G-d said to him, "I do not want the death of the wicked, but since you do want to lose your world, then go with them."

Why did Rashi apply the midrash to a later verse than the one used by the midrash itself?

The story of Bilam dithering over whether or not to curse Israel contains several stages; G-d agrees that Balaam can go with the messengers both in verse 20 and verse 35. The midrash comments on the first time, while Rashi uses the midrash for his comment on the second time.

Why? After G-d consents the first time, He still puts obstacles in Bilam's way. Only in verse 35 is Bilam really led to go where he desires to go, and therefore Rashi used the midrash on this verse.

The midrash, on the other hand, wanted to teach the principle of "One is led to go the way one chooses to go" and the basis for this lesson was stated even on the first verse because we see there that Bilam wanted to go and G-d agreed.

We see again the "division of labor" between Rashi and the Midrash. The Midrash utilizes a verse to teach a principle; Rashi uses a midrash to explain a verse.

One more example should show that we are dealing with a systematic approach by Rashi. In Bereishit chapter 33, Yaakov prepares his family to meet his brother Esav, whom he hadn't seen in over twenty years. He fears Esav's anger, and therefore arranges his wives and children in a way to protect his most loved relatives.

BEREISHIT 33:2

וַיָּשֶׂם אֶת־הַשְּׁפָחוֹת וְאֶת־יַלְדֵיהֶן רִאשֹׁנָה וְאֶת־לֵאָה וִילָדֶיהָ אַחֲרֹנִים וְאֶת־רָחֵל וְאֶת־יוֹסֵף אַחֲרֹנִים:

And he placed the maidservants and their children first; *and Leah and her children last*, and Rachel and Yoseph last.

RASHI

ואת לאה וילדיה אחרונים: אחרון אחרון חביב.

And Leah and her children last: The further back, the more beloved.

This is a strange comment! Rashi makes this brief comment, taken from a midrash in *Bereishit Rabba*, on the words "Leah and her children last." He seems to be saying that Leah, and not Rachel, was Yaakov's most beloved – but the Torah itself testifies that ויאהב גם את רחל מלאה, "he loved Rachel more than Leah" (Bereishit 29:30). As we saw in chapter 3, Rashi understands "last" to mean "latter" here; he is explaining why the Torah refers to Leah as "last" even though Rachel and her children come after her.

Since we are interested here in Rashi's use of Midrash, let us see the midrash that was Rashi's source:

BEREISHIT RABBA 78:8

וישם את השפחות ואת ילדיהן ראשונה וגו'...ואת רחל ואת יוסף אחרונים*: הדא אמרה, "אחרון אחרון חביב."

And he placed the maidservants and their children first... and Rachel and Yoseph last: This is as it is said, "The further back, the more beloved."

We see from this midrash that Rashi got the concept of אחרון אחרון חביב from here. The words before the colon are the *dibbur hamatchil*; they are the Torah's words. But the midrash quotes only the beginning and the end of the verse – it skips the words "and Leah and her children last." In other words, it specifically skips the words that Rashi comments on! What is the meaning of this difference between the emphasis of the midrash and that of Rashi?

The reason, we again stress, is that Rashi and Midrash have different "agendas," different goals. The Midrash's goal was to use the verse to teach a lesson – moral, spiritual or psychological – so all it needed to quote were words that showed that there was an ascending order in the position of Yaakov's wives – first was the least beloved, last was the most beloved. But Rashi, on the other hand, uses Midrash to explain difficulties in the Torah's words. So Rashi quoted only the problematic words – "Leah and her children last" – which he explains with his comment.

---

* This *dibbur hamatchil* is from the scholarly and accurate edition of *Midrash Rabba: Bereishit* by Moshe Aryeh Mirkin. Most editions have a different *dibbur hamatchil*.

This is another example of Rashi using the Midrash to explain different words than the ones that the Midrash itself chose.

IV. Rashi Changes the Wording of the Midrash

Sometimes Rashi will quote a midrash but in the process will change a word or two of the midrash's original wording. Some might attribute this slight change to a lapse of memory on Rashi's part. We disagree with this easy answer, for the following reasons. For one, Rashi in his comprehensive Talmud commentary also quotes other Talmudic texts and midrashim. In that commentary he always quotes them precisely. It is not reasonable that he would be less precise in his Torah commentary. Furthermore, Rashi quotes midrashim entirely correctly, other than a word or two. Such selective "forgetting" makes it unlikely to be accidental. And finally, when we investigate these apparent "lapses of memory" we discover that there is method to them. It is then that we realize how Rashi has applied his creative touch to his Midrash-based comments.

An example of this can be found in Vayikra 26:8. The verse is part of the blessings bestowed on the people, which precedes a litany of curses if they should fail to keep G-d's word.

וְרָדְפוּ מִכֶּם חֲמִשָּׁה מֵאָה וּמֵאָה מִכֶּם רְבָבָה יִרְדֹּפוּ וְנָפְלוּ אֹיְבֵיכֶם לִפְנֵיכֶם לֶחָרֶב:

And *five of you* will pursue one hundred, *and a hundred of you* will pursue *ten thousand*. And your enemies will fall before you by the sword.

RASHI

חמשה מאה ומאה מכם רבבה: וכי כך הוא החשבון, והלא לא היה צריך לומר אלא מאה מכם שני אלפים ירדופו. אלא אינו **דומה מועטין העושין את התורה למרובין העושין את התורה**.

Five [of you] will pursue one hundred, and a hundred of you will pursue ten thousand: But is that [the correct] number? Should it not have said "a hundred of you, two thousand"? Rather, *there is no comparison between the few who fulfill the Torah to the many who fulfill the Torah.*

Rashi points out the discrepancy in ratios in our verse. Five to a hundred works out to a ratio of one to every twenty. That being the case, one hundred soldiers should pursue twenty times their number, i.e., two thousand – not ten thousand as the verse says.

Rashi explains that the numbers do not multiply simply, they multiply exponentially. This, he explains, is because there is no comparison between the few and the many when it comes to Torah observance.

But the midrash in *Torat Kohanim* (2:10) actually says:

ומאה מכם רבבה: וכי כך הוא החשבון? והלא לא היה צריך לומר אלא "מאה מכם שני אלפים ירדופו"? אלא אין דומה המרובים העושים את התורה למועטים העושים את התורה.

One hundred of you ten thousand: But is that [the correct] number? Should it not have said "a hundred of you will pursue two thousand"? But there is no comparison *between the many who fulfill the Torah to the few who fulfill the Torah.*

If you look closely you will see that Rashi changed the midrash's wording. The midrash mentioned "the many" before "the few"; Rashi reversed the order.

Why did he make this change? The reason would seem to be that Rashi was following the order of the words as they were in the Torah. The Torah listed the numbers from lowest to highest: 5, 100; 100, 10,000. The Torah listed the lower numbers first, but the midrash refers first to the greater numbers. Rashi therefore reversed the midrash's order to fit the Torah's words more precisely.

Rashi followed the wording of the midrash precisely *except* where he wanted to make a change. Again we see that Rashi is using a midrashic insight to fit the Torah's words.

v. Rashi Combines Two Separate Midrashim

Rashi will sometimes combine words from two separate midrashim to create an original aphorism. See the example below:

SHEMOT 19:2

וַיִּסְעוּ מֵרְפִידִים וַיָּבֹאוּ מִדְבַּר סִינַי וַיַּחֲנוּ בַּמִּדְבָּר וַיִּחַן־שָׁם יִשְׂרָאֵל נֶגֶד הָהָר:

And they journeyed from Rephidim and they came to the Wilderness of Sinai, *and Israel encamped there* opposite the mountain.

RASHI

ויחן שם ישראל: כאיש אחד בלב אחד, אבל שאר כל החניות בתערומות ובמחלוקת.

And Israel encamped there: As one man with one heart. But all their other encampments were accompanied by murmuring and dissension.

Rashi's midrashic source is the *Mechilta* (*Ba'chodesh* 1):

ויחן שם ישראל: כל מקום שהוא אומר "ויסעו" "ויחנו" – נוסעים במחלוקת וחונים במחלוקת. אבל כאן השוו לב אחד, לכך נאמר, "ויחן שם ישראל כנגד ההר".

And Israel encamped there: Wherever it says "and *they* journeyed," "and *they* encamped," it indicates that they were journeying with dissension and they were encamping with dissension, but here it says "and Israel encamped [singular] there" indicating that they were *all of one heart.*

Do you see any difference between the wording in the midrash and Rashi's wording?

There are several differences. But what is crucial is that the midrash says "with one heart" while Rashi says "as one man, with one heart." Rashi added the words "as one man"; it is Rashi's own, original phrase.

This is not unintentional. For if we look at another well-known Rashi comment we find a similar word change:

SHEMOT 14:10

וּפַרְעֹה הִקְרִיב וַיִּשְׂאוּ בְנֵי־יִשְׂרָאֵל אֶת־עֵינֵיהֶם וְהִנֵּה מִצְרַיִם נֹסֵעַ אַחֲרֵיהֶם וַיִּירְאוּ מְאֹד וַיִּצְעֲקוּ בְנֵי־יִשְׂרָאֵל אֶל ה':

And Pharaoh came near and the Children of Israel raised their eyes and behold Egypt *was traveling after them* and they were very frightened and the Children of Israel called out to Hashem.

RASHI

נוסע אחריהם: בלב אחד, כאיש אחד.

[Egypt] was traveling after them: With one heart, as one man.

The midrashic source for this is also in the *Mechilta* (*Vaychi* 2):

והנה מצרים נוסע אחריהם: "נוסעים" אין כתיב כאן, אלא "נוסע" – מגיד שנעשו כלן תורמיות תורמיות כאיש א'.

[Egypt] was traveling after them: It does not say "*were* traveling" [plural] but "*was* traveling" [singular]. This tells us that the Egyptians all formed squadrons, each [marching] *as one man.*

Again we find the strange phenomenon – Rashi expands on the words of the midrash. *The midrash has only "as one man"; Rashi has "with one heart, as one man."* Rashi had turned a simple two-word explanation into a memorable aphorism.

Once we see Rashi's midrashic sources we can understand

the answer to a question that has puzzled many students. The question has been asked: Why did Rashi switch the word order in these two comments; in one he wrote "with one heart, as one man" and in the other he wrote "as one man, with one heart"? This seems quite arbitrary. But when we see the midrashim on which these comments are based, we can understand. The Egyptian army was waging a military battle against the Israelites. Manly strength was the important factor. There the Midrash says "as one man." When the Israelites stood at Mount Sinai, waiting to receive the Torah, it was spirituality, matters of the heart, that were central. There the Midrash says "with one heart."

Rashi added his own touch by poeticizing these simple terms. He strengthened the Midrash's words and bolstered them by adding two Hebrew words. To the Midrash's "as one man" he added "with one heart." To the Midrash's "with one heart" he added "as one man." With this slight emendation Rashi transformed the Midrash's phrase into a popular proverb.

VI. Rashi Creates His Own Midrash

Of the various ways of Rashi with Midrash, we find a particularly astonishing phenomenon – at times Rashi constructed, or we should say reconstructed, his own midrash! Certainly this is not a frequent occurrence in his commentary, but we can find at least one such instance of this. Analyzing this comment gives us insight into Rashi's thinking.

I am referring to the Rashi in Bereishit 27:45. There the Torah tells of Rivka's words to Yaakov as she sends him off to her brother Lavan, to get away from Esav:

BEREISHIT 27:45

עַד־שׁוּב אַף־אָחִיךָ מִמְּךָ וְשָׁכַח אֵת אֲשֶׁר־עָשִׂיתָ לּוֹ וְשָׁלַחְתִּי וּלְקַחְתִּיךָ מִשָּׁם לָמָה אֶשְׁכַּל גַּם־שְׁנֵיכֶם יוֹם אֶחָד:

Until your brother's anger against you subsides and he forgets what you have done to him, then I will send and bring you from there; why should I be bereaved of *both of you* on the same day?

RASHI

גם שניכם: אם יקום עליך ואתה תהרגו יעמדו בניו ויהרגוך. ורוח הקודש נזרקה בה ונתנבא שביום אחד ימותו, כמו שמפורש בפרק המקנא לאשתו.

Both of you: [She said] "Should he [Esav] rise up against you [Yaakov] and you kill him, then his children will rise up and kill you." Here [Rivka] had an inspiration of the Holy Spirit and she prophesied that they would both die on the same day, as is explained in the chapter "*Hamekanei l'Ishto*" (*Sota* 13a).

When we check Rashi's source in *Sota* 13a, we find something very different from what Rashi has told us. There the Talmud elaborates at length on the events that occurred when the sons of Yaakov came to bury him in Kiryat Arba. The Talmud relates that Esav refused to allow them to bury Yaakov in one of the two remaining plots allotted to Yitzchak's son and wife. Esav claimed the plot for himself. He said that while Yaakov had indeed purchased the firstborn's portion, that portion had already been used by Yaakov when he buried Leah there. Yaakov's sons said that Esav had sold Yaakov both plots and they had the deed to prove it. Esav demanded to see the deed, but since it was kept in Egypt, Naftali, the swiftest runner, had to run and fetch it. During this whole, protracted argument, Yaakov lay exposed without burial. Dan's deaf son, Chushim, demanded to understand why Yaakov's honor was assaulted in this way. When he learned of Esav's obstinacy, he rose and killed Esav. The Talmud concludes by saying: "At that moment Rivka's prophecy was fulfilled, as it says, 'Why should I be bereaved of both of you on the same day?'"

As can be seen by comparing this *aggada* with Rashi's comment, this is a much different tale than the one Rashi tells us. Rashi said that Esav might attack Yaakov, and Yaakov would overcome him and kill him, whereupon Esav's sons would kill Yaakov, thus both dying the same day as Rivka had feared. But the Midrash says that Yaakov's grandson killed Esav during Yaakov's burial, thus both dying the same day. Why did Rashi ignore the story of the *aggada* and make up his own story?

We cannot say that Rashi is actually referring to an unknown midrash that has been lost over the years, because Rashi himself tells us the source of this story – *Sota* 13a. The reason Rashi didn't choose the events as recounted in the Talmud should be clear once we think about it. Those events took place long after Rivka had died, when Yaakov was 180 years old. Rashi could not use the Talmud's story to explain the words "why should I *be bereaved* of both of you…" A parent is only "bereaved" when the child dies during the parent's own lifetime, not after the parent himself has died. That is not considered bereaved, for it is quite natural for children to die *after* their parents have died. So Rashi had to construct a case in which they both would die in the near future, during Rivka's lifetime.

Now let us look closely at the scenario Rashi constructed. It is a convoluted case in which Esav rises up against Yaakov (soon after Yaakov stole the blessings), but Yaakov, in self-defense, kills Esav. Why not have Esav kill Yaakov right off? That is really what Rivka feared. If you think about it, you can understand why Rashi was forced to make up the case as he did. Let us explore the alternative possible scenarios.

1. Esav kills Yaakov in anger for stealing the blessings. But then who will kill Esav in revenge? Remember, we need a case where they both die on the same day. Yaakov had not yet married; he had no children who would kill Esav in defense of their father's honor. So this possibility must be rejected.

2. Yaakov rises up and kills Esav; then Esav's children take revenge and kill Yaakov. Here we have a case in which both die. But why would Yaakov kill Esav? He had no reason to kill him. So this possibility must be rejected.

The only way a case can be constructed is as Rashi constructed it – Esav, in anger, rises up against Yaakov, but (and here's the twist) Yaakov overpowers Esav and kills him in self-defense. Then Esav's children take revenge and kill Yaakov. In this case, and only in this case, can we reasonably conceive of them both dying on the same day during Rivka's lifetime.

We see Rashi's thinking here. He took the core idea of the midrash – that they both died on the same day and thus Rivka's prophecy is fulfilled – yet he had to construct his own midrash to fit the words of the Torah.

Chapter 6
Rashi's *Dibbur Hamatchil*

A little-studied aspect of Rashi's Torah commentary is his lead words, *dibbur hamatchil*. These are the words from the Torah text that Rashi comments on. In our printed *chumashim* they are printed in bold letters. It seems from old manuscripts that Rashi himself chose the *dibbur hamatchil*; it is not the printer's choice.

Sometimes these *dibbur hamatchil*s are important for understanding deeper meanings in Rashi's comment. We will see some examples to illustrate this point.

1. A *Dibbur Hamatchil* to Open Each Parasha

Rashi begins every parasha with lead words that contain the name of the parasha. He does this apparently to delineate where a new parasha begins. This means that Rashi may have a lead word at the beginning of the parasha even though he has no comment to make on the words. This is quite obvious and easy enough to verify. Nevertheless some commentators are not aware of this. So, for example, we find commentators trying to explain Rashi's *dibbur hamatchil* on parashat Vayeilech, where all he writes is וילך וגו' with no comment. Some commentators, unaware of this characteristic of Rashi's commentary, have attempted to explain what Rashi means by not commenting on these words even though he writes them as a *dibbur hamatchil*. As we said, no explanation is necessary or called for here.

Other examples of a *dibbur hamatchil* at the beginning of a parasha without a subsequent comment are found in Bereishit 44:18; Shemot 13:17, 27:20; Devarim 11:26, 26:1, 31:1 and 33:1. The only exception to this that I am aware of is parashat Kedoshim, where Rashi comments on other words before his comment on the word "Kedoshim," which is the name of the parasha.

It should be noted that Rashi (and also Tosephot) has the same in rule in his commentary on the Talmud. Each chapter begins with a *dibbur hamatchil* that contains the name of the chapter even if he has no comment on those words. This too may have been done to enable the student to know where a new chapter begins.

II. A *Dibbur Hamatchil* to Open Each *Chumash*

Rashi begins every new *chumash* with a *dibbur hamatchil* containing the first word of the first verse. Look at the five verses that begin a new sefer and the Rashi comment on each one. Notice closely the *dibbur hamatchil* of each Rashi comment.

In addition to noting the *dibbur hamatchil*, notice also that the first comment of each of the five books of the Torah contains the idea of G-d's love of Israel or of His land of Israel or of His prophet, Moshe. This is Rashi's way of inspiring his students as they learn the Torah.

BEREISHIT 1:1

בְּרֵאשִׁית בָּרָא אֱלֹקִים אֵת הַשָּׁמַיִם וְאֵת הָאָרֶץ:

In the beginning G-d *created* the heavens and the earth.

RASHI

בראשית ברא: אמר רבי יצחק: לא היה צריך להתחיל [את] התורה אלא מ"החודש הזה לכם" (שמות יב:ב), שהיא מצווה ראשונה שנצטוו [בה] ישראל, ומה טעם פתח בבראשית? משום "כוח מעשיו הגיד לעמו לתת להם נחלת גויים" (תהילים קיא:ו), שאם יאמרו אומות העולם לישראל לסטים אתם, שכבשתם

ארצות שבעה גויים, הם אומרים להם כל הארץ של הקב״ה היא, הוא בראה ונתנה לאשר ישר בעיניו, ברצונו נתנה להם וברצונו נטלה מהם ונתנה לנו.

In the beginning He created: Rabbi Yitzchak said: He should have begun the Torah from "This is for you the first month" (Shemot 12:2), for that is the first mitzva that Israel was commanded. So what is the reason it began with the Creation? Because it says, "He declared the power of His works to His people in order to give them the inheritance of nations" (Tehillim 111:6). For if the nations say to Israel, "You are robbers, since you conquered the lands of seven nations," they can answer them, "The entire world belongs to the Holy One; He created it and gave it to whomever He saw fit. It was His desire to give it to them and it was His will to take it from them and gave it to us."

SHEMOT 1:1

וְאֵלֶּה שְׁמוֹת בְּנֵי יִשְׂרָאֵל הַבָּאִים מִצְרָיְמָה אֵת יַעֲקֹב אִישׁ וּבֵיתוֹ בָּאוּ:

And these are the names of the Children of Israel who came to Egypt: every man and his household came with Yaakov.

RASHI

ואלה שמות בני ישראל: אף על פי שמנאן בחייהן בשמותן, חזר ומנאן במיתתן [אחר מיתתן], להודיע חבתן שנמשלו לכוכבים, שמוציאן ומכניסן במספר ובשמותם, שנאמר, "המוציא במספר צבאם לכולם בשם יקרא" (ישעיהו מ:כו).

And these are the names of the Children of Israel: Even though He had counted them in their lifetime with their names, nevertheless He counted them again, as it says, "He brings out in number their hosts; to all of them, He calls by name" (Yeshayahu 40:26).

VAYIKRA 1:1

וַיִּקְרָא אֶל־מֹשֶׁה וַיְדַבֵּר ה' אֵלָיו מֵאֹהֶל מוֹעֵד לֵאמֹר:

And Hashem called to Moshe, and spoke to him out of the Tent of Meeting, saying....

RASHI

ויקרא אל משה: לכל דברות ולכל אמירות ולכל ציוויים קדמה קריאה, לשון חבה, לשון שמלאכי השרת משתמשים בו, שנאמר, "וקרא זה אל זה" (ישעיה ו:ג), אבל לנביאי אומות העולם נגלה עליהן בלשון עראי וטומאה, שנאמר, "ויקר אלוקים אל בלעם" (במדבר כג:ד).

And Hashem called to Moshe: All "speakings" and all "sayings" and all "commands" are preceded by a call. This is a term of endearment; it is the term that the angels use, as it says, "And they *called* one to another..." (Yeshayahu 6:3). But to the prophets of the gentiles He is revealed in a term of impurity and temporality, as it says, "And G-d happened upon Bilam" (Bamidbar 23:4).

BAMIDBAR 1:1

וַיְדַבֵּר ה' אֶל־מֹשֶׁה בְּמִדְבַּר סִינַי בְּאֹהֶל מוֹעֵד בְּאֶחָד לַחֹדֶשׁ הַשֵּׁנִי בַּשָּׁנָה הַשֵּׁנִית לְצֵאתָם מֵאֶרֶץ מִצְרַיִם לֵאמֹר:

And Hashem *spoke* to Moshe *in the Wilderness of Sinai*, in the Tent of Meeting, *on the first* day *of the* second *month*, in the second year after they had come out of Egypt, saying....

RASHI

וידבר. במדבר סיני. באחד לחדש וגו': מתוך חיבתן לפניו מונה אותם כל שעה. כשיצאו ממצרים מנאן, וכשנפלו בעגל מנאן לידע מניין הנותרים. כשבא להשרות שכינתו עליהן מנאן: באחד בניסן הוקם המשכן, ובאחד באייר מנאם.

And He spoke. In the Wilderness of Sinai. On the first of the month: Because of His love of them, He counted them at every opportunity. When they left Egypt, He counted them; when they fell after the sin of the Golden Calf, He counted them to know the number that remained. When He came to rest his *Shechina* on them He counted them: on the first of the month of Nissan the Sanctuary was erected and on the first of the month of Iyar [the following month] He counted them.

DEVARIM 1:1

אֵלֶּה הַדְּבָרִים אֲשֶׁר דִּבֶּר מֹשֶׁה אֶל־כָּל־יִשְׂרָאֵל בְּעֵבֶר הַיַּרְדֵּן בַּמִּדְבָּר בָּעֲרָבָה מוֹל סוּף בֵּין־פָּארָן וּבֵין־תֹּפֶל וְלָבָן וַחֲצֵרֹת וְדִי זָהָב:

These are the words that Moshe spoke to all of Israel beyond the Jordan, in the wilderness, in the plain opposite the Red Sea, between Paran and Tophen and Lavan and Chatzerot and Di Zahav.

RASHI

אלה הדברים: לפי שהן דברי תוכחות ומנה כאן כל המקומות שהכעיסו לפני המקום בהן. לפיכך סתם את הדברים והזכירם ברמז מפני כבודן של ישראל.

These are the words: Because these are words of reproof, He recounted here all the places that they angered Him. Therefore He mentioned them only in hints out of respect for the honor of Israel.

We see that every *dibbur hamatchil* that opens a new book of the Torah contains the first word in the verse and includes the name of the parasha (as Rashi does for the beginning of each parasha). In all five *chumashim*, the name of the *chumash* and the name of the parasha is one and the same.

But notice Rashi's strange *dibbur hamatchil* on the opening to Bamidbar. It has three separate parts:

1. וידבר: This is the first word of the *dibbur hamatchil* because it is a new book of the Torah; there is no need for Rashi to comment on it.
2. במדבר סיני: This is part of the *dibbur hamatchil* because it contains the name of the parasha; there is no need for Rashi to comment on it, either.
3. באחד לחדש וגו': Only on these words does Rashi have a comment.

Once we know that Rashi brings the *dibbur hamatchil* for the first words of each *chumash* and for each parasha name, the above comment will not fluster us. We understand that Rashi intentionally quoted the first words of the *chumash* and the parasha name without commenting; his first comment appears on the first words in the verse that pose a difficulty.

III. Discrepancies between the *Dibbur Hamatchil* and the Verse

Sometimes the *dibbur hamatchil* is slightly different than the Torah's words. This is important to note because it helps us understand Rashi's comment.

BEREISHIT 32:16

גְּמַלִּים מֵינִיקוֹת וּבְנֵיהֶם שְׁלֹשִׁים פָּרוֹת אַרְבָּעִים וּפָרִים עֲשָׂרָה אֲתֹנֹת עֶשְׂרִים וַעְיָרִם עֲשָׂרָה:

Nursing camels and their offspring, thirty; forty cows, ten oxen, twenty she-donkeys and ten he-donkeys.

RASHI

גמלים מיניקות שלשים: ובניהם עמהם.

Nursing camels thirty: and their offspring with them.

Look closely – here Rashi uses the words of the verse but changes their order, and then he adds one word of his own: עמהם (with them). He does this to clarify what is not clear from the Torah's words.

What is not clear? The Torah says "nursing camels and their offspring, thirty...." The question is: Were there thirty mother camels together with their offspring or were there thirty mother camels in addition to their offspring?

The way Rashi arranges his *dibbur hamatchil* makes it clear – there were thirty mother camels *together* with their offspring. Another example:

BEREISHIT 1:4

וַיַּרְא אֱלֹקִים אֶת־הָאוֹר כִּי־טוֹב וַיַּבְדֵּל אֱלֹקִים בֵּין הָאוֹר וּבֵין הַחֹשֶׁךְ:

And G-d saw that the light was good, and G-d separated between the light and the darkness.

RASHI

וירא אלוקים את האור כי טוב ויבדל: אף בזה אנו צריכים לדברי אגדה. ראהו שאינו כדאי להשתמש בו רשעים והבדילו לצדיקים לעתיד לבא.

ולפי פשוטו כך פרשהו ראהו כי טוב ואין נאה לו ולחשך שיהיו משתמשין בערבוביא, וקבע לזה תחומו ביום ולזה תחומו בלילה.

And G-d saw that the light was good, and G-d separated: Also for this we need the words of the *aggada*. He saw that it was not fitting for the evil ones to use [the light], so He set it aside [separated it] for the righteous to use in the World to Come.

But according to the *pshat*, He saw that it was good, and that it was not right for it and the darkness to be mixed together. Thus He set this [i.e., the light] to be in the day and this [i.e., the darkness] to be at night.

In this verse, the *etnachta* – which functions like a comma – appears below the word "good" (*tov*). Rashi's *dibbur hamatchil* connects the words before the *etnachta* with the word after it, thereby ignoring the *etnachta* break. Rashi then offers a *pshat* interpretation which considers the *etnachta*.

Chapter 7
Rashi and the Rashbam

Rashi was the moving force behind a crucial turning point in the history of Torah interpretation. It was Rashi who placed *pshat* interpretation "on the map."* But he wasn't the "last word" in *pshat* interpretation. His grandson Rabbi Shmuel ben Meir, known as the Rashbam, took this trend even further than Rashi did. The Rashbam tells us that his commentary will emphasize the *pshat* interpretations. In his Torah commentary, the Rashbam makes us privy to a discussion between himself and his famous grandfather.

In a beginning comment to Vayeshev (Bereishit 37:2), the Rashbam writes:

> Be wise and understand, those who love reason, what our rabbis taught us "that no verse abandons its simple [*pshat*] meaning" (*Shabbat* 63a). It is true that the essence of the Torah comes to teach and make us aware by hints of *pshat* and *aggadot* and the laws and rules by means of

---

* In actuality the Sephardi scholars were the very first to embark on *pshat* interpretation. Saadia Gaon (b. Egypt, 882; d. Baghdad, 942) translated the Torah into Arabic, and his translation was characterized by *pshat*. Menachem ibn Saruk (920–970) of Spain wrote a biblical dictionary called the *Machberet*, which is basic to understanding the *pshat* meaning of the Torah's words. Rashi made use of this dictionary. But since Rashi's commentary was the most accepted both in northern Europe and in Arabic countries, it was he who made *pshat* interpretation popular.

extended language and by means of the thirty-two rules of Rabbi Eliezer the son of Rabbi Yossi Hagelili and by the thirteen rules of Rabbi Yishmael. The *rishonim*, due to their righteousness, dealt mainly with *drashot* which are the main [part of the Torah]. And because of this they weren't accustomed to probe the depth of *pshat* of the Torah.... And because of this they did not accustom themselves very much to the *pshat* of the verses. As it says in tractate *Shabbat*, "I was eighteen years old and had learned the whole Talmud but I did not know that a verse never abandons its simple [*pshat*] meaning." Rabbi Shlomo [Rashi], my mother's father, who illuminated the eyes of the Diaspora, who wrote commentaries on the Torah, the Prophets and the Writings [Tanach], set out to explain the plain meaning of the Scripture. However, I, Shmuel, son of his son-in-law Meir, zt"l, often argued with him and he admitted to me that if only he had had the time, *he would have written new commentaries, based on the insights into the plain meaning of Scripture* [pshat] *that are newly thought of day by day.*...

We discussed this revealing Rashbam comment in chapter 2. What concerns us here is that the Rashbam was more focused on *pshat* than Rashi was and he disputed Rashi many times on such issues. From their very first comments in Bereishit we can already see the difference between their approaches.

Different Approaches to *Pshat*

Rashi's first comment is famous. In it he asks (quoting a midrash) why the Torah did not begin with the first laws addressed to the Jewish nation, i.e., those laws in Shemot 12 where the laws of Passover are discussed, instead of telling us about Creation and the lives of the forefathers. Rashi's answer is:

"He declared the power of His works to His people in order to give them the inheritance of nations" (Tehillim 111:6). For if the nations say to Israel, "You are robbers, since you conquered the lands of seven nations," they [Israel] can answer them, "The entire world belongs to the Holy One; He created it and gave it to whomever He saw fit. It was His desire to give it to them and it was His will to take it from them and give it to us."

The Rashbam also has a long comment on this verse. By stressing "true *pshat*" in his opening phrase, he is clearly rejecting Rashi's comment:

> The following is the true *pshat* of our text, which follows the scriptural pattern of regularly anticipating and explaining some matter which, though unnecessary to the immediate context, serves the purpose of elucidating some matter to be mentioned later on in another passage.
> For example, when the text writes "Shem, Cham and Yephet" (Bereishit 9:18), why does it then proceed to write "Cham is the father of Canaan"? It is because it is written below, "Cursed is Canaan" (Bereishit 9:25). Had we not known before who Canaan was, we would not have understood why Noach cursed him....
> This entire section, concerning the six days of Creation, was also written by Moshe for anticipatory purposes, so as to explain to the reader what G-d said when He gave the Torah: "Remember the Sabbath day and keep it holy...for in six days Hashem made the heaven and earth and sea, and all that is in them, and He rested on the seventh day" (Shemot 20:8–11).

We see that the Rashbam understands that the reason for the

Torah beginning with the Creation story was only to prepare us for understanding the fourth commandment to keep the Sabbath.

In their different comments on this verse, Rashi and the Rashbam have highlighted different approaches to *pshat* interpretation in general. The Rashbam has given us a technical answer to the question Rashi posed – why the Torah, a book of law, began with the Creation story. The Rashbam tells us that his interpretation is strict *pshat*, in the sense that he builds on the literary style of the Torah, i.e., the anticipation of information, unnecessary now but necessary for understanding a verse later on in the Torah. Rashi, on the other hand, uses his comment not just to answer the question in a technically correct way, but also to inspire his students and bolster their belief in the justice of the Jews being the rightful owners of the Holy Land. He wrote the comment at the time of the First Crusade, when Christians were claiming ownership of the Holy Land.

Another example of the Rashbam differing from Rashi can be seen in these beginning comments on Creation. Both Rashi and the Rashbam interpret the unusual *"hei hayedia"* (article) in the words *"the* sixth day":

BEREISHIT 1:31

וַיַּרְא אֱלֹקִים אֶת־כָּל־אֲשֶׁר עָשָׂה וְהִנֵּה־טוֹב מְאֹד וַיְהִי־עֶרֶב וַיְהִי־בֹקֶר **יוֹם הַשִּׁשִּׁי**:

And G-d saw all that He had made and it was very good; and it was evening and it was morning, *the sixth day*.

RASHI

יום הששי: הוסיף ה"א בששי, בגמר מעשה בראשית, לומר שהתנה עמהם על מנת שיקבלו עליהם ישראל חמשה חומשי תורה.

דבר אחר: יום הששי, שכלם תלוים ועומדים עד יום הששי, הוא ששי בסיון. וזהו יום הששי בה"א, שאותו יום ו' בסיון המוכן למתן תורה.

The sixth day: He added the *hei* to the sixth day at the end of the creative process, to say that He made the existence of the created world conditional on Israel's acceptance of the five [*hei*] books of the Torah.

Another interpretation: *The* sixth day, for all [of Creation] was suspended until the sixth day, which was the sixth of Sivan. That is [the meaning of] *"the* sixth day" – the sixth of Sivan, which was prepared for the giving of the Torah.

The Rashbam gives a different, less midrashic interpretation of the extra *hei*:

> That is what it says "And it was evening and it was morning, *the* sixth day." That same sixth day that was the end of the six days [of Creation], which the Holy One referred to at the giving of the Torah.

We see how these two commentators interpret the *"hei hayedia"* in their characteristic ways – Rashi relied on Midrash, while the Rashbam strove for *pshat* based on his literary technique of "anticipatory information."

Professor Meir Lockshin pointed out another example of the difference between the commentaries of Rashi and the Rashbam. The Torah discusses the case of a servant who wants to remain a servant after his six-year mandatory period of servitude has ended.

SHEMOT 21:5–6

וְאִם־אָמֹר יֹאמַר הָעֶבֶד אָהַבְתִּי אֶת־אֲדֹנִי אֶת־אִשְׁתִּי וְאֶת־בָּנָי לֹא אֵצֵא חָפְשִׁי: וְהִגִּישׁוֹ אֲדֹנָיו אֶל־הָאֱלֹהִים וְהִגִּישׁוֹ אֶל־הַדֶּלֶת אוֹ אֶל־הַמְּזוּזָה וְרָצַע אֲדֹנָיו אֶת־אָזְנוֹ בַּמַּרְצֵעַ וַעֲבָדוֹ לְעֹלָם:

And if the servant says, "I love my master, my wife and my children; I will not go out free." Then his master shall bring him to the judges and draw him near the door or doorpost and *his master shall bore his ear with the awl* and he will serve him forever.

Rashi comments:

ורצע אדניו את אזנו במרצע: ומה ראה אוזן להרצע מכל שאר אברים שבגוף? אמר רבי יוחנן בן זכאי (קדושין כב:): אוזן זאת ששמעה על הר סיני לא תגנוב, והלך וגנב, תרצע. ואם מוכר עצמו, אוזן ששמעה על הר סיני "כי לי בני ישראל עבדים" (ויקרא כה:נה), והלך וקנה אדון לעצמו, תרצע.
ר' שמעון היה דורש מקרא זה כמין חומר, מה נשתנו דלת ומזוזה מכל כלים שבבית? אמר הקב"ה: דלת ומזוזה שהיו עדים במצרים כשפסחתי על המשקוף ועל שתי המזוזות ואמרתי כי לי בני ישראל עבדים – עבדי הם ולא עבדים לעבדים – והלך זה וקנה אדון לעצמו, ירצע בפניהם.

And his master should bore his ear with the awl: What is it about the ear that it should be bored more than other limbs of the body? Rabban Yochanan ben Zakkai said: The ear that heard at Mount Sinai "You shall not steal," yet he went and stole – let it be bored. And if he sold himself – the ear that heard at Mount Sinai "For to Me are the Children of Israel servants," yet this one went and willingly bought himself a master – let it be bored.

Rabbi Shimon explained the verse as a string of pearls [beautifully]: How are a door and a doorpost unique of all the vessels in the house? The Holy One said: "The door and the doorpost were witnesses in Egypt when I passed over the lintel and the two doorposts [of the Israelites] and said, 'For to Me are the Children of Israel servants' – they are My servants and not the servants of servants. Yet this one purchased a master for himself – let him be bored before them."

The Rashbam offers a very different comment on this verse:

Door and doorpost: Even if the house is of stone, these are made of wood and can thus be bored through ear and door.

The Rashbam offers a very simple, even prosaic comment – if the house was made of stone, we couldn't bore through it, and therefore the doorpost was chosen since it is made of wood, which is soft enough to be bored through.

The commentaries differ strikingly – the Rashbam offers a no-frills, down-to-earth explanation for boring the ear in the doorpost. Rashi, on the other hand, makes use of the midrash to teach us a moral lesson – man should only be G-d's servant, never a servant to another man.

We can learn from these examples something central to Rashi's commentary. While Rashi's commentary does emphasize *pshat*, it is no less a vehicle for teaching and inspiring one in Torah values – it is not *just* a commentary.

Rashi-Rashbam Disputes

Let us look at some Rashi-Rashbam disputes in commentary. We will see the Rashbam's strivings for pure *pshat*, and we will explore how Rashi could stand up to the Rashbam's criticism.

BEREISHIT 34:25

וַיְהִי בַיּוֹם הַשְּׁלִישִׁי בִּהְיוֹתָם כֹּאֲבִים וַיִּקְחוּ שְׁנֵי־בְנֵי־יַעֲקֹב שִׁמְעוֹן וְלֵוִי אֲחֵי דִינָה אִישׁ חַרְבּוֹ וַיָּבֹאוּ עַל־הָעִיר **בֶּטַח** וַיַּהַרְגוּ כָּל־זָכָר:

And it was on the third day when they were in pain that two of Yaakov's sons, Shimon and Levi, Dina's brothers, each took his sword and they came upon the city *confidently* [Hebrew: בֶּטַח] and killed all the males.

RASHI

בטח: שהיו כואבים. ומדרש אגדה: בטוחים היו על כחו של זקן.

Confidently [בֶּטַח]: Because they [the inhabitants of Shechem] were in pain. The *midrash aggada* says that they were confident in the power of the elder [Yaakov].

THE RASHBAM

They came upon the city: Who were dwelling בֶּטַח and were not careful of them. And likewise every use of בֶּטַח, whether in the Torah or Prophets, always refers to the dwellers. Both in the Torah [see Devarim 12:10, 28:52, 33:28] and in the Prophets [see Shoftim 8:11 and Yechezkel 30:9].

The Rashbam disagrees with Rashi on the *pshat* interpretation of the word בטח. The Rashbam bolsters his claim that "securely" refers to the dwellers of Shechem and not to Shimon and Levi (as Rashi maintains) by citing other places in Tanach where the word בטח refers to the dwellers of the city. It is the Rashbam's style to cite similar instances in Tanach of a word that he is commenting on in order to demonstrate its meaning.

This sounds convincing, but is it? Why would Rashi, who certainly knew the verses the Rashbam cited, nevertheless say it was Shimon and Levi who were "confident"?

Note two things here. Firstly, it is obvious that the dwellers would be confident. Why shouldn't they be confident? What should they be afraid of? They had fulfilled Yaakov's conditions and had no reason to suspect that Yaakov or his sons would wreak havoc on them. So it is unnecessary for the Torah to mention this. On the other hand, it would be important for the Torah to tell us that the two young boys, Shimon and Levi, had the courage and confidence to attack a whole city.

Secondly, Rashi tells us why they were confident – because the people of Shechem were in pain from undergoing circumcision. There is an unwritten rule in *pshat* interpretation that if two facts are mentioned in the same verse then they are probably related to each other. Our verse begins by telling us that on the third day the people of Shechem were in pain and then it tells of Shimon and Levi approaching the city בֶּטַח. It would thus seem that the pain of the dwellers gave Shimon and Levi confidence.

So even on the *pshat* level, Rashi can hold his own when the Rashbam differs.

Another example:

SHEMOT 22:21–23

כָּל־אַלְמָנָה וְיָתוֹם לֹא תְעַנּוּן: אִם־עַנֵּה תְעַנֶּה אֹתוֹ כִּי אִם־צָעֹק יִצְעַק אֵלַי שָׁמֹעַ אֶשְׁמַע צַעֲקָתוֹ: וְחָרָה אַפִּי וְהָרַגְתִּי אֶתְכֶם בֶּחָרֶב **וְהָיוּ נְשֵׁיכֶם אַלְמָנוֹת** וּבְנֵיכֶם יְתֹמִים:

Every widow or orphan you shall not oppress. If you oppress them, if he will cry out to Me, I will certainly listen to his outcry. My wrath will glow and I will kill you by the sword *and your wives will be widows* and your children, orphans.

RASHI, SHEMOT 22:23

והיו נשיכם אלמנות: ממשמע שנאמר "והרגתי אתכם", איני יודע שנשיכם אלמנות ובניכם יתומים?! אלא הרי זו קללה אחרת, שיהיו הנשים צרורות כאלמנות חיות, שלא יהיו עדים למיתת בעליהן ותהיינה אסורות להינשא. והבנים יהיו יתומים, שלא יניחום בית דין לירד לנכסי אביהם לפי שאין יודעים אם מתו אם נשבו.

And your wives will be widows: Since it says "I will kill them" wouldn't I know that their wives would be widows and their children will be orphans? But this is an additional curse that their wives will be bound up like widows from the living [unable to marry], for there will be no witnesses of the husband's death and they will thus be forbidden to marry. And their children will be orphans, in that the courts will not allow them to take possession of their father's property because they don't know if the father is dead or in captivity.

Rashi, in his conviction that no words in the Torah are redundant, asks why we have to be told that a woman whose husband was killed is a widow and her children are orphans. That is by definition so! To explain the apparent redundancy, Rashi (based on a midrash) tells us that the phrase "widows and orphans" is an additional punishment, i.e., the woman will be a "living widow" (agunah), meaning that since the death of her husband cannot be verified she may not remarry. And the children will be unverified orphans and cannot inherit their father, since it is not certain that he is dead.

THE RASHBAM

And your wives will be: [This is] measure for measure.

The Rashbam, on the other hand, is not troubled by the redundancy. Its purpose, he seems to say, is to emphasize the "measure for measure" nature of the punishment. The oppressor of widows will end up being killed, such that his own wife will become a widow. Thus the "redundancy" is there for a purpose – it spells out the obvious in order to emphasize the poetic justice that G-d metes out.

We see how Rashi and the Rashbam illustrate two different approaches to interpretation. There is a debate in the Talmud (*Berachot* 31b): one opinion is that "the Torah speaks in the language of men"; the other view is the opposite – the Torah has its own style, according to which every word has its own significance. The opinion that "the Torah speaks in the language of men" means that just as ordinary people may repeat words for emphasis, without necessarily attributing any additional meaning to the redundant words, so too the Torah may say things that seem redundant in order to emphasize a point. This is what the Rashbam is saying here. The use of the words "widow" and "orphans" for the wife and children of a deceased man are redundancies used to point out the fair "measure for measure" character of this punishment. Rashi, on the other hand, looks for the additional lesson of these extra words, for the Torah's language is unique and not as ordinary man's speech.

Let us look at another verse on which Rashi and the Rashbam differ. When Moshe pleads with G-d to have mercy on the people after the sin of the Golden Calf, Moshe says:

SHEMOT 32:32

וְעַתָּה אִם־תִּשָּׂא חַטָּאתָם וְאִם־אַיִן מְחֵנִי נָא מִסִּפְרְךָ אֲשֶׁר כָּתָבְתָּ:

Now if You would bear their sin, but if not, then erase me *from Your book* which You have written.

RASHI

מספרך: מכל התורה כולה, שלא יאמרו עלי שלא הייתי כדאי לבקש עליהם רחמים.

From Your book: From the whole Torah. So they should not say that I wasn't worthy enough to demand mercy for them.

THE RASHBAM

From Your book: From the Book of Life that You wrote, as it says, "All who are written for life in Jerusalem" (Yeshayahu 4:3) [and] "Kill me, please, kill me" (Bamidbar 11:15).

The Rashbam, as we have seen, searches through the Tanach to find similar ideas or words that could shed light on our verse. First he finds that there is such a concept as writing someone for life, so "erase me from Your book" could signify a request to be erased from the Book of Life. Then he fortifies his interpretation that Moshe requested that G-d kill him by citing another verse in the Torah in which Moshe explicitly asked this of G-d.

The Rashbam's interpretation seems to be stronger than Rashi's here. Rashi posits that Moshe is asking to be erased from the Torah – but what is the value of that? In Rashi's defense we could say that the Torah is called a book in several places in the Torah, and it is that which Rashi draws from. His way is to look at the verse and the surrounding context. Just a few chapters previously the Torah is called the Book of the Covenant.

SHEMOT 24:7

וַיִּקַּח סֵפֶר הַבְּרִית וַיִּקְרָא בְּאָזְנֵי הָעָם וַיֹּאמְרוּ כֹּל אֲשֶׁר דִּבֶּר ה' נַעֲשֶׂה וְנִשְׁמָע:

And he took the Book of the Covenant and he called in the ears of the people and they said, "All that Hashem spoke we shall do and we shall hear."

Rashi also explains the point of Moshe's request: "So they should not say that I wasn't worthy enough to demand mercy for them."

In sum: It is hard to say here which interpretation is the closest to *pshat*; they both have justifications. But we can discern the preferences of each commentator. The Rashbam prefers to search throughout the Tanach to understand the Torah text, while Rashi is more focused on the verse and its surroundings.

Another example of their differing interpretations:

VAYIKRA 23:42–43

בַּסֻּכֹּת תֵּשְׁבוּ שִׁבְעַת יָמִים כָּל־הָאֶזְרָח בְּיִשְׂרָאֵל יֵשְׁבוּ בַּסֻּכֹּת: לְמַעַן יֵדְעוּ דֹרֹתֵיכֶם כִּי **בַסֻּכּוֹת הוֹשַׁבְתִּי** אֶת־בְּנֵי יִשְׂרָאֵל בְּהוֹצִיאִי אוֹתָם מֵאֶרֶץ מִצְרָיִם:

You shall dwell in booths seven days; every citizen in Israel shall dwell in booths. So your generations will know *that*

> *I made* the Children of Israel *dwell in booths* when I took them out of the land of Egypt.
>
> RASHI, VAYIKRA 23:43
>
> כי בסכות הושבתי: ענני כבוד.
>
> **I made dwell in booths:** In Clouds of Glory.
>
> THE RASHBAM
>
> **So your generations will know:** The *pshat* is in actual booths.

This dispute between Rashi and the Rashbam is a dispute in the Talmud (*Succah* 11b). The Rashbam chooses the naturalistic interpretation: the booths that the Israelites dwelt in while they were in the wilderness were actual, humanly constructed booths. Rashi chose the less naturalistic interpretation: the booths here are the Clouds of Glory that traveled with the people during the years in the wilderness.

Which interpretation is *pshat*? Although the Rashbam's choice of a naturalistic interpretation would seem to be closest to *pshat*, the matter is not that simple. The Torah mentions G-d's cloud that traveled with the people several times. One of the times it says:

> BAMIDBAR 14:14
>
> וְאָמְרוּ אֶל־יוֹשֵׁב הָאָרֶץ הַזֹּאת שָׁמְעוּ כִּי־אַתָּה ה' בְּקֶרֶב הָעָם הַזֶּה: אֲשֶׁר־עַיִן בְּעַיִן נִרְאָה אַתָּה ה' וַעֲנָנְךָ עֹמֵד עֲלֵהֶם וּבְעַמֻּד עָנָן אַתָּה הֹלֵךְ לִפְנֵיהֶם יוֹמָם וּבְעַמּוּד אֵשׁ לָיְלָה.
>
> And they will say about the inhabitants of this land, "They have heard that You, Hashem, appeared eye to eye and Your cloud stands over them and in a pillar of cloud You go before them by day and in a pillar of fire by night."

Thus, there is scriptural evidence that G-d's cloud protected the people.

Another point favoring Rashi is the word הושבתי ("I made dwell"). This transitive verb fits better when we think of G-d making us dwell in His cloud than if the Israelites themselves built their own booths and dwelt in them on their own initiative.

The Ramban adds another point supporting Rashi's view. After quoting Rashi he says:

> In my opinion it is correct that this is the *pshat*. For G-d had commanded that the generations should know all G-d's actions which He had done for them wondrously.

Ramban is saying that if these were actual, humanly built booths then there is nothing special for generations to remember. But if these were G-d's Clouds of Glory which He granted the people, it would certainly be important for future generations to be aware of this.

Considering all these points it would seem that in spite of Rashi choosing a supernatural interpretation, understanding the booths as the Clouds of Glory still seems more like *pshat* than the Rashbam's naturalistic interpretation.

Chapter 8

Questioning Rashi: An Important Key

The key to probing Rashi's deeper meaning is by asking questions on his comments. The reason for this is that we have a basic assumption regarding his commentary: *Rashi only comments when there is a need to clarify matters*. It is the student's job to figure out what needs to be clarified. This simple axiom is what enables us to unlock the treasures in Rashi's commentary. This may seem obvious at first glance, but most students learn Rashi without this in mind and they consequently never fully understand him nor realize his genius.

As we approach Rashi with questions, it is important to keep the following point in mind. The English word "question" has two equivalents in Hebrew: one is שאלה, which means a question; the other is קושיא, which means "difficulty." The best way to show the difference between a שאלה and a קושיא is to recall the four קושיות that the child asks at the Pesach Seder. They are קושיות and not שאלות. The child does not ask "Why do we eat matza on Pesach?" – that would be a שאלה. Instead he asks "On all other nights we eat chametz and matza but on this night we eat only matza." There is an apparent contradiction here between tonight and all other nights; thus this is a קושיא. As we will see, we only ask difficulties on Rashi, not questions. Students sometimes ask:

Why didn't Rashi comment on this verse? That is a שאלה but not a קושיא. Rashi is not obligated to comment on every verse in the Torah. We have no way of knowing why he didn't comment on a particular verse. On the other hand, it is appropriate to ask a קושיא. When, for example, we see a contradiction in Rashi this is cause for asking: Why does he seem to contradict himself? I will suggest some typical questions and give examples of how they open up Rashi comments to deeper analysis.

1. Why Does Rashi State the Obvious?

When Rashi's comment seems obvious and states what we could have known even without the comment, our question is: Why does he tell us the obvious?

Example no. 1

This example comes from the story of Yoseph and his brothers. They stand before the Egyptian viceroy, not knowing that he is Yoseph, their long-lost brother.

BEREISHIT 42:21–23

וַיֹּאמְרוּ אִישׁ אֶל־אָחִיו אֲבָל אֲשֵׁמִים אֲנַחְנוּ עַל־אָחִינוּ אֲשֶׁר רָאִינוּ צָרַת נַפְשׁוֹ בְּהִתְחַנְנוֹ אֵלֵינוּ וְלֹא שָׁמָעְנוּ עַל־כֵּן בָּאָה אֵלֵינוּ הַצָּרָה הַזֹּאת: וַיַּעַן רְאוּבֵן אֹתָם לֵאמֹר הֲלוֹא אָמַרְתִּי אֲלֵיכֶם לֵאמֹר אַל־תֶּחֶטְאוּ בַיֶּלֶד וְלֹא שְׁמַעְתֶּם וְגַם־דָּמוֹ הִנֵּה נִדְרָשׁ: וְהֵם לֹא יָדְעוּ כִּי שֹׁמֵעַ יוֹסֵף **כִּי הַמֵּלִיץ בֵּינֹתָם**:

> And each man said to his brother: "But we are guilty regarding our brother when we saw the distress of his soul when he pleaded with us but we didn't listen. Therefore this trouble has come upon us." And Reuven answered them saying: "Did I not say, 'Don't sin against the boy' – and also his blood is being requited." But they didn't know that Yoseph was listening, *for the interpreter was between them.*

RASHI, BEREISHIT 42:23

כי המליץ בינתם: כי כשהיו מדברים עמו היה המליץ ביניהם היודע לשון עברי ולשון מצרי, והיה מליץ דבריהם ליוסף ודברי יוסף להם. לכך היו סבורים שאין יוסף מכיר בלשון עברי.

> **For the interpreter was between them:** For when they had spoken to him there was an interpreter between them who knew both the Hebrew and the Egyptian languages. He interpreted their words to Yoseph and Yoseph's words to them. Consequently they were under the impression that Yoseph did not understand the Hebrew language.

What has Rashi told us that we didn't know before? He explains that the interpreter was necessary because the Egyptian viceroy (Yoseph) spoke to them in Egyptian, while they spoke only Hebrew. The question is: What has this comment added to our understanding?

Here is where we ask: What is bothering Rashi? What is difficult in our verse that requires a comment?

Our verse reads: "But they didn't know that Yoseph was listening [understood], for the interpreter was between them." But that makes no sense – if the interpreter was there, then Yoseph would certainly understand what they were saying thanks to his interpreter! So why does it say that they didn't know that Yoseph understood? This is Rashi's implicit question.

When we read Rashi carefully we see his insight. He writes *"when they had spoken* to him there was an interpreter..." Rashi is telling us that previously there had been an interpreter present, indicating that Yoseph did not understand their language. That was in the past but now the interpreter was *not* present, so they could speak freely. So the words כי המליץ בינתם ("the interpreter *was* between them") means he had been between them in the past. Now, however, he was not between them. This is what Rashi is teaching us.

In this way the verse makes sense, overcoming the difficulties we posed. In his effortless manner, Rashi points out the correct meaning of the verse.

Example no. 2

This example comes from parashat Noach, where we learn the seven Noachide Laws. The particular law discussed is the prohibition of murder and its punishment:

BEREISHIT 9:6

שֹׁפֵךְ דַּם הָאָדָם בָּאָדָם דָּמוֹ יִשָּׁפֵךְ כִּי בְּצֶלֶם אֱלֹקִים עָשָׂה אֶת־הָאָדָם:

He who spills the blood of a man, *by man his blood shall be spilled*: for in the image of G-d, He made man.

RASHI

באדם דמו ישפך: אם יש עדים המיתוהו אתם. למה? "כי בצלם אלקים" וגו'.

By man his blood shall be spilled: If there were witnesses you shall kill him. Why? Because "in the image of G-d..."

Rashi says we must kill the man who killed another man because the victim was made *in the image of G-d*. In other words, the reason the murderer is sentenced to the death penalty is because he killed a human being, who was made in the image of G-d. If one kills a rabbit or a cow, one is not punished; one is only punished for killing a human because the human alone was made in the image of G-d.

But this is exactly what the verse tells us. What has Rashi added to our understanding? This, then, is our question: What is Rashi teaching us?

Note that this comment is a Type II comment (see chapter 3), which means there is not necessarily a difficulty in the verse; Rashi is helping us avoid a misunderstanding.

Let us analyze this to discover Rashi's unstated question. The verse before this one also condemns a killer to death. There it says:

BEREISHIT 9:5

וְאַךְ אֶת־דִּמְכֶם לְנַפְשֹׁתֵיכֶם אֶדְרֹשׁ מִיַּד כָּל־חַיָּה אֶדְרְשֶׁנּוּ וּמִיַּד הָאָדָם מִיַּד אִישׁ אָחִיו אֶדְרֹשׁ אֶת־נֶפֶשׁ הָאָדָם:

But your blood which belongs to your souls I will demand, of every beast will I demand it, and of man, of every man from that of his brother, I will demand the soul of man.

Rashi comments on this verse, explaining that it is referring to a situation in which there were no witnesses to a murder. Because of this there can be no case before a *beit din* and therefore the verse says "I will punish him" meaning that G-d Himself will punish the murderer.

With this in mind we can suggest that Rashi is wondering why verse 5 didn't say that the murderer is killed "because in the image of G-d He made him," as is stated in verse 6. The only difference between the two verses is that verse 6 speaks of murder *with witnesses* where judges kill him and the previous verse speaks of murder *without witnesses* where G-d kills him. But in both cases the murderer is condemned to death, so in both cases it is appropriate to add that he is killed "because in the image of G-d..." But the first verse did not add these words – why not? That is Rashi's implicit question.

Notice Rashi asks: "...you shall kill him. Why?" It is unusual for Rashi to ask a question openly as he does here. He does so here because he wants to stress a point: His question is "Why do *you* – a human court – kill him?" The implication is: What right does one person have to kill another human being? G-d may kill as punishment, for He gives life and He can take life (as in the previous verse), but by what right does man have that awesome privilege as well? And then comes Rashi's (surprising) answer: "*Because in the image of G-d, He made him.*" Meaning G-d made *the judge* in the image of G-d and therefore he has the right to enforce capital punishment.

Now it makes sense why the words "because in the image of G-d He made him" are attached to this verse and not the previous verse, because only here do they tell us a new insight. Thus Rashi is really telling us something we would not have understood from a superficial reading of the verse, and we discovered this only because we asked a question on this comment.

Example no. 3

The following is an example of a comment that seems quite banal and lacking in any significance. It invites us to ask: Why does Rashi comment here?

SHEMOT 12:30

וַיָּקָם פַּרְעֹה לַיְלָה הוּא וְכָל־עֲבָדָיו וְכָל־מִצְרַיִם וַתְּהִי צְעָקָה גְדֹלָה בְּמִצְרָיִם כִּי־אֵין בַּיִת אֲשֶׁר אֵין־שָׁם מֵת׃

And Pharaoh rose up at night, he and all his servants and all of Egypt and there was a great outcry in Egypt, because there was no house that did not have a death.

RASHI

ויקם פרעה: ממטתו.

And Pharaoh rose: from his bed.

Such a mundane comment! What purpose is there to Rashi's one-word comment "from his bed"? It seems so unimportant and so self-understood. Of course Pharaoh got up from his bed, but why tell us that?

But remember, Rashi never comments unnecessarily. The word ויקם means to rise up or to get up. But in biblical Hebrew it has another meaning as well. It may mean the person did something with forethought and intentionality, but not necessarily that he physically got up. An example comes from:

BEREISHIT 4:8

וַיָּקָם קַיִן אֶל־הֶבֶל אָחִיו וַיַּהַרְגֵהוּ:

And Kayin rose up and killed Hevel his brother.

"Rose up" here does not mean he physically got up. That is unimportant; it means he acted with premeditation.

Another example:

SHEMOT 2:17

וַיָּקָם מֹשֶׁה וַיּוֹשִׁעָן וַיַּשְׁקְ אֶת־צֹאנָם:

And Moshe rose up and saved them and watered their sheep.

Here too the meaning of ויקם is not that Moshe physically got up, but that he acted with forethought and determination.

But how are we to know when ויקם means to get up physically or when it means to act with forethought?

The answer is that when the verb ויקם is followed by another verb (like וַיַּהַרְגֵהוּ or וַיּוֹשִׁעָן) then it means to act with forethought; but when it is not followed by another verb it means literally to get up. In our verse ויקם is *not* followed by another verb, so Rashi concluded it means that Pharoah got up physically from his bed. Rashi was not just telling us what Pharaoh did; he also indirectly taught a rule of biblical grammar.

Example no. 4

This difficult Rashi comment is found at the beginning of parashat Bamidbar. There Hashem tells Moshe to appoint princes for each of the twelve tribes. The names of each prince and his tribe are listed. Then the Torah says the following:

BAMIDBAR 1:17

וַיִּקַּח מֹשֶׁה וְאַהֲרֹן אֵת הָאֲנָשִׁים הָאֵלֶּה אֲשֶׁר נִקְּבוּ בְּשֵׁמוֹת:

And Moshe and Aharon took *these men who were designated by name*.

RASHI

האנשים האלה: את שנים עשר נשיאים הללו.
אשר נקבו: כאן בשמות.

These men: These twelve princes.
Who were designated: here by name.

This short comment has puzzled all the Rashi commentaries. The problem is that Rashi tells us nothing new; he says just what the Torah itself said! Rashi tells us that the words "these men" refer to the twelve princes just listed. Of course, that's obvious! This is a perfect example of Rashi apparently telling us what we already know. So we ask: Why did Rashi make the comment?

Note that this is a Type II comment. Rashi weaves his words in between the Torah's words.

The Mizrachi offers the following explanation. He writes that since the Torah had just listed the men, it should have stated that Moshe and Aharon took "them," rather than "these men." But since the Torah did say "these men" and not "them" I might have thought that the Torah was referring to other men who were not listed here. So therefore Rashi comes and sets us straight: "these men" does not mean other men; it means "the twelve princes who were designated here."

But that answer is problematic. Because if, in the final analysis, "these men" are the same as those listed, then we again ask: Why doesn't the Torah just say "take *them*" instead of "take these men"?

The Gur Aryeh offers another answer. His answer is that Rashi says "these twelve *princes*." Rashi wants us to know that when the Torah said "these men" they were not ordinary men – they were princes. But this too is problematic, because if that is what the Torah meant – it should have said "these princes" and not "these men."

We must look elsewhere for an adequate explanation of this seemingly simple Rashi. We note that Rashi uses the word נשיאים, "princes"; this should ring a bell. So we ask: When was the last time the Torah referred to these princes? We do not find these "princes" mentioned in the whole book of Vayikra. But we do find them in the book of Shemot:

SHEMOT 35:27

וְהַנְּשִׂאָם הֵבִיאוּ אֵת אַבְנֵי הַשֹּׁהַם וְאֵת אַבְנֵי הַמִּלֻּאִים לָאֵפוֹד וְלַחֹשֶׁן:

The princes brought the *shoham* stones and the *miluim* stones for the *ephod* and the *choshen*.

This verse is very helpful because these stones had engraved on them the names of the twelve tribes. While the Torah does not tell us which tribes were engraved, Rashi does:

SHEMOT 28:10

שִׁשָּׁה מִשְּׁמֹתָם עַל הָאֶבֶן הָאֶחָת וְאֶת־שְׁמוֹת הַשִּׁשָּׁה הַנּוֹתָרִים עַל־הָאֶבֶן הַשֵּׁנִית כְּתוֹלְדֹתָם:

Six of their names on one stone and the names of the six remaining ones on the second stone *according to the order of their birth*.

RASHI

כתולדותם: כסדר שנולדו: ראובן שמעון לוי יהודה דן נפתלי, על האחת, ועל השניה גד אשר יששכר זבולן יוסף בנימין מלא, שכן הוא כתוב במקום תולדתו. עשרים וחמש אותיות בכל אחת ואחת.

According to the order of their birth: In the order that they were born: Reuven, Shimon, Levi, Yehuda, Dan, Naftali on one stone; and on the second stone Gad, Asher, Yissachar, Zevulun, Yoseph, Binyamin. There were twenty-five letters on each side.

Here Rashi tells us what names were on the stones, implying that it was the princes of these tribes who brought the stones.

But when we compare these tribes with the tribes listed in Bamidbar we realize that these were not the same twelve tribes! Our list has Ephraim and Menashe and does not have Levi, while the list in Shemot has Yoseph and Levi.

Now we can understand the simple truth of Rashi's comment in Bamidbar. Rashi makes us aware that this list of tribes is *not* the original list. *This is the first time in the Torah* that Ephraim and Menashe are included and Yoseph and Levi are excluded from the list of twelve tribes.

Now we see the precision of Rashi's words. "These [and not the original] twelve princes, who were designated here by name [as opposed to the verse in Shemot, where they were not designated by name in the Torah]."

The point of this Rashi, which has puzzled so many, is quite simple and straightforward. Rashi was alert to the difference in the list of tribes, though most students would not be. I see this Rashi comment and its simple explanation as evidence that Rashi always has a simple message, even if we cannot see it right off.

Another example of Rashi telling us the obvious is his comment on Bereishit 48:16. This has stumped many Rashi commentators. We analyzed this Rashi comment above (see chapter 5, section II, "Rashi Rejects a Midrash").

11. Why Does Rashi Reject the Straightforward Meaning?

When Rashi's comment seems to go against the apparent meaning of the verse, we must ask: Why does Rashi interpret the verse differently than the straightforward meaning?

Example no. 1
The following example shows us how correct questioning reveals a very subtle point.

VAYIKRA 26:6–7

וְנָתַתִּי שָׁלוֹם בָּאָרֶץ וּשְׁכַבְתֶּם וְאֵין מַחֲרִיד וְהִשְׁבַּתִּי חַיָּה רָעָה מִן הָאָרֶץ וְחֶרֶב לֹא תַעֲבֹר בְּאַרְצְכֶם: וּרְדַפְתֶּם אֶת אֹיְבֵיכֶם וְנָפְלוּ לִפְנֵיכֶם לֶחָרֶב:

And I will give peace in the land, and you will lie down without fear and I will cause the evil beast to cease from the land and a sword will not pass through your land. And you will pursue your enemies and they will fall *before you by the sword*.

RASHI, VAYIKRA 26:7

לפניכם לחרב: איש בחרב רעהו.

Before you by the sword: Each man by the sword of his friend.

The apparent meaning of this verse is that Israel's enemies will fall before them as Israel kills its enemy, yet Rashi gives us a very different interpretation. He interprets our verse to mean that Israel's enemies will fall by the sword of their fellow soldiers, which is called "friendly fire." This is by no means the apparent meaning of these words. Our question is: Why does Rashi choose a meaning that is at odds with the plain sense of the verse?

The Torah's idiom of לפי חרב contains a subtle message nearly impossible to discern. There is a little-known language rule in the

Torah: whenever Israel wages war against a gentile enemy the Torah uses the words לפי חרב, but when non-Jews wage war the language is always לחרב. Our verse has the term לחרב, which is used when the gentiles wage war. This indicates that the killing done here is by a gentile, not by a Jew. Again, the discovery of this nuance in the Torah's words was possible only once we questioned Rashi's comment.

We must try to understand the meaning of the difference between לפי חרב and לחרב. When the Jews wage war, the Torah uses the term לפי חרב (literally "by the mouth of the sword"), possibly because the Jews first pray to Hashem before they use the sword in battle. On the other hand, when the gentiles wage war, prayer is not an essential aspect of their battle plan and therefore the language is just לחרב.

Example no. 2

This example comes from the story of Moshe and the Cushite woman he married. We will see how Rashi seems to say just the opposite of what the Torah says.

BAMIDBAR 12:1

וַתְּדַבֵּר מִרְיָם וְאַהֲרֹן בְּמֹשֶׁה עַל־אֹדוֹת הָאִשָּׁה הַכֻּשִׁית אֲשֶׁר לָקָח כִּי־אִשָּׁה כֻשִׁית לָקָח:

And Miriam and Aharon spoke against Moshe regarding the matter of the Cushite woman whom he had taken, *for a Cushite woman he had taken.*

RASHI

כי אשה כשית לקח: ועתה גרשה.

For a Cushite woman he had taken [married]: And now he divorced her.

The Torah says Moshe married this woman; Rashi says he married her and then divorced her!

Such a comment certainly deserves a question: Why should Rashi uproot the basic meaning here?

What would you ask?

One question that one can ask on the verse is as follows: The verse appears to be repetitious. First it says "the matter of the Cushite woman whom he had taken." Then it repeats *"for* a Cushite woman he had taken." The implicit question is: Why the repetition?

How does Rashi's comment deal with the repetition? What is your answer?

An answer: The second phrase comes to teach us something. Rashi tells us it teaches us that he had married the Cushite woman but then divorced her. The possible reason for Rashi's comment could be that the repetition is a way of "protesting too much." In other words, by repeating the fact of the marriage the Torah actually conveys the opposite message – that Moshe divorced her.

We see how noticing a Rashi comment that seems to say the opposite of what the Torah says is grounds for questioning the comment. In doing this we uncover the deeper reason behind the comment.

Example no. 3

The following is an example of a Rashi comment that seems to say the opposite of what the Torah says. It is from the story of Yitzchak and his dispute with Avimelech, the king of the Philistines.

BEREISHIT 26:15–18

וְכָל־הַבְּאֵרֹת אֲשֶׁר חָפְרוּ עַבְדֵי אָבִיו בִּימֵי אַבְרָהָם אָבִיו סִתְּמוּם פְּלִשְׁתִּים וַיְמַלְאוּם עָפָר: וַיֹּאמֶר אֲבִימֶלֶךְ אֶל־יִצְחָק לֵךְ מֵעִמָּנוּ כִּי־עָצַמְתָּ מִמֶּנּוּ מְאֹד: וַיֵּלֶךְ מִשָּׁם יִצְחָק וַיִּחַן בְּנַחַל־גְּרָר וַיֵּשֶׁב שָׁם: וַיָּשָׁב יִצְחָק וַיַּחְפֹּר אֶת־בְּאֵרֹת הַמַּיִם אֲשֶׁר חָפְרוּ בִּימֵי אַבְרָהָם אָבִיו וַיְסַתְּמוּם פְּלִשְׁתִּים אַחֲרֵי מוֹת אַבְרָהָם וַיִּקְרָא לָהֶן שֵׁמוֹת כַּשֵּׁמֹת אֲשֶׁר־קָרָא לָהֶן אָבִיו:

And all the wells that his father's servants had dug in the days of his father Avraham the Philistines stuffed up and filled with earth. And Avimelech said to Yitzchak, "Go from us! Because you have become much stronger than us." And Yitzchak went from there and he encamped in the Valley of Gerar and settled there. *And* Yitzchak *returned and dug* wells of water which had been dug in the days of Avraham his father but the Philistines had stuffed them up after Avraham died. And he called their names after the names that his father had called them.

RASHI, BEREISHIT 26:18

וישב... ויחפר: הבארות אשר חפרו בימי אברהם אביו. ופלשתים סתמום, מקודם שנסע יצחק מגרר חזר וחפרן.

And he returned... and he dug: The wells which were dug in the days of Avraham, his father. But the Philistines stuffed them up, before Yitzchak went from Gerar he returned and dug them.

As we look at this comment notice the emphasized words; they are the Torah's words. Actually Rashi just seems to be quoting the Torah except for his last words – "before Yitzchak went from Gerar he returned and dug them." These are Rashi's words and they are quite strange. How could Yitzchak "return" to dig wells even "before he went from Gerar"? You cannot return to a place before you left it! Another difficulty is that this contradicts what the Torah says. Verse 17 says Yitzchak "went from there" (leaving Gerar) and verse 18 says he "returned and dug..." Rashi says he dug *before* he left the place!

How can these contradictions be resolved? This is clearly a case of Rashi apparently contradicting what the Torah said.

All becomes clear the moment we understand that in biblical Hebrew the meaning of the word וישב has two possible meanings:

1) to physically return to a place; 2) to redo an action. The word וישב here bears the second meaning: "Yitzchak *dug again* the wells that his father had dug."

So we translate the last phrase in Rashi differently. Now it reads: "before Yitzchak went from Gerar he redug them." So he didn't return to a place he had not yet left! We also have to correct the translation of the *dibbur hamatchil* (lead words), which now reads "And he re-dug."

How does one know if the word וישב means to return or to redo? The answer is simple. If וישב is followed by a place, like וישב ראובן אל הבור, "And Reuven returned to the pit" then means to return; but if it is followed by another verb then it means to redo that verb.

Note Rashi's lead words and see something interesting. The lead words are וישב...ויחפר – the word יצחק is missing. Why?

It would seem that Rashi is alerting us to the fact that וישב is followed by another verb "to dig" indicating that it means to "dig again."

So though at first it looked like Rashi was going against the words of the verse, upon closer examination it turns out not to be so. Our questioning led to a new understanding of the Torah's words.

III. Why Does Rashi Offer Both *Pshat* and *Drash*?

Rashi will occasionally give two interpretations, one *pshat* and one *drash*. In such cases we should ask: Why the need for the second interpretation, the *drash*? Similarly, when Rashi provides two *pshat* interpretations we should question why he brought both.

Example no. 1

This example is from the story of Shimon and Levi who avenge the shame of their sister Dina and destroy the city of Shechem. (We explored one aspect of Rashi's comment in chapter 7 above, where we contrasted Rashi's comment with that of the Rashbam.)

BEREISHIT 34:25

וַיְהִי בַיּוֹם הַשְּׁלִישִׁי בִּהְיוֹתָם כֹּאֲבִים וַיִּקְחוּ שְׁנֵי־בְנֵי־יַעֲקֹב שִׁמְעוֹן וְלֵוִי אֲחֵי דִינָה אִישׁ חַרְבּוֹ וַיָּבֹאוּ עַל־הָעִיר **בֶּטַח** וַיַּהַרְגוּ כָּל־זָכָר:

And it was on the third day when they were in pain that two of Yaakov's sons, Shimon and Levi, Dina's brothers, each took his sword and they came upon the city *confidently* and killed all the males.

RASHI

בטח: שהיו כואבים. ומדרש אגדה: בטוחים היו על כחו של זקן.

Confidently: Because they [the inhabitants of Shechem] were in pain. The *midrash aggada* says that they were confident in the power of the elder [Yaakov].

Here Rashi offers two interpretations. 1) The *pshat* interpretation is that Shimon and Levi were confident because their intended victims were in pain and too weak to defend themselves. 2) The second interpretation Rashi labels as *drash*. Their confidence came from their trust in the strength of Yaakov.

Our question should be: The *pshat* seems to explain matters adequately; why do we need the midrash? In such cases, where Rashi offers both *pshat* and *drash*, we look for reasons why the *pshat* did not fully explain matters. Regarding this Rashi comment the commentators point out that the fact the men of Shechem were in pain is not sufficient. What if the surrounding cities heard of the slaughter and then attacked Yaakov? In fact this is exactly what Yaakov says to Shimon and Levi in verse 30.

Therefore Rashi brought the midrash to explain their confidence that Yaakov would protect them in spite of the neighbor's threat.

Let us look at another example of a Rashi comment with both *pshat* and *drash* in it.

Example no. 2

In chapter 12 of Shemot we are told the laws of Pesach. The first law has to do with sanctifying the first month of the year, Nissan – the month in which Pesach falls.

SHEMOT 12:2

הַחֹדֶשׁ הַזֶּה לָכֶם רֹאשׁ חֳדָשִׁים רִאשׁוֹן הוּא לָכֶם לְחָדְשֵׁי הַשָּׁנָה:

This month is for you the first of the months; it is first for you of the months of the year.

RASHI

החדש הזה: הראהו לבנה בחידושה ואמר לו כשהירח מתחדש יהיה לך ראש חודש. ואין מקרא יוצא מידי פשוטו. על חדש ניסן אמר לו, זה יהיה ראש לסדר מנין החדשים, שיהא אייר קרוי שני, סיון שלישי.

This month: He showed him the moon in its renewal and said to him "When the moon renews itself it will be for you Rosh Chodesh." *But a verse never loses its plain sense [pshat].* [Therefore the meaning is] regarding the month of Nissan He said to him, "This will be the first in the order of the months, thus Iyar will be called the second; Sivan called the third.

Rashi gives us *drash* and then *pshat*, insisting that a verse never loses its *pshat* meaning. The question we pose is: If Rashi had *pshat* why give us *drash* at all?

He must have felt the *pshat* was in some way deficient.

The weakness of the *pshat* should be self-evident. The second half of the verse explicitly states that this month is the first of the year's months – so why have the message repeated? For this reason Rashi also gave us the *drash*; in the *drash* the two halves of the verse have different messages and are thus not redundant.

But he had to give the simple *pshat* because "no verse loses its *pshat* meaning."

Example no. 3

BEREISHIT 6:13

וַיֹּאמֶר אֱלֹקִים לְנֹחַ קֵץ כָּל־בָּשָׂר בָּא לְפָנַי כִּי־מָלְאָה הָאָרֶץ חָמָס מִפְּנֵיהֶם וְהִנְנִי מַשְׁחִיתָם אֶת־הָאָרֶץ:

And G-d said to Noach: "The end of all flesh has come before Me, because the earth is filled with violence due to them; and I will destroy them *with the Earth*."

RASHI

את הארץ: כמו מן הארץ. ודומה לו: "כצאתי את העיר" (שמות ט:כט) – מן העיר, "חלה את רגליו" (מ"א טו:כג) – מן רגליו. דבר אחר: את הארץ – עם הארץ, שאף שלושה טפחים של עומק המחרישה נימוחו וניטשטשו.

[את] **the earth:** Meaning "from the earth." Similarly "when I go out [את] of the city" (Shemot 9:29); "sick [את] from his legs" (1 Melachim 15:23).

Another interpretation: [The words] את הארץ means "with the earth" – even three *tefachim*, the depth of plowing, was disintegrated and destroyed.

We wonder why Rashi needed two interpretations. Both are based on reasonable translations of the Hebrew word את – that word does mean both "with" and "from." The *Maskil L'David* suggests that the first interpretation is weak because nothing would be lacking had the words את הארץ not been added. Of course all living beings were exterminated "from the earth" – those words add nothing to our understanding. So we need the second interpretation. But the second interpretation is also somewhat problematic, because it claims that the earth was destroyed with (at the same time as) the people. But this is not so. The living creatures died by drowning as soon as the water reached a certain height; but the earth was destroyed somewhat later, as the water seeped into the earth.

Example no. 4

In the following comment Rashi offers both *pshat* and another interpretation which is a midrash, though Rashi does not label it so. We have seen this comment in chapter 5 above, as an example of Rashi selecting one midrash from among many.

BEREISHIT 27:1

וַיְהִי כִּי־זָקֵן יִצְחָק וַתִּכְהֶיןָ עֵינָיו מֵרְאֹת וַיִּקְרָא אֶת־עֵשָׂו בְּנוֹ הַגָּדֹל וַיֹּאמֶר אֵלָיו בְּנִי וַיֹּאמֶר אֵלָיו הִנֵּנִי:

And it was when Yitzchak became old and his eyes *were dimmed* from seeing and he called to Esav his older son and he said, "My son," and he said to him, "Here I am."

RASHI

ותכהין: בעשנן של אלו שהיו מעשנות ומקטירות לעבודה זרה. דבר אחר: כדי שיטול יעקב את הברכות.

[His eyes] **were dimmed:** Because of the smoke of these [women] who would burn incense for idol worship.

Another explanation: To enable Yaakov to receive the blessings.

The questions we ask are: Why the need for another interpretation in addition to *pshat*? And why does Rashi offer the midrashic interpretation *before* the *pshat*, even though we know he prefers *pshat* to *drash*?

We look for weaknesses in each of these interpretations to justify Rashi's use of both of them. Reading the verse carefully we realize that the *drash* is weak because the words "and it was when Yitzchak grew old" in the verse are irrelevant, because the reason for his blindness was the smoke of idol worship and not his old age. So Rashi also brought *pshat*: Yitzchak's eyes were dimmed by old age to enable Yaakov to receive the blessings. But what is weak about the *pshat* – why couldn't he just offer the *pshat* without the *drash*?

An explanation given for this is that the words "from seeing" in the verse appear less relevant to the *pshat* than they are to the *drash*. The *drash* is that his eyes were dim from seeing the idol worship of his son's wives. This answer translates the word *"from seeing"* to mean *due* to seeing and not from *being able* to see.

The *drash* is based on this verse's proximity to the previous verse, which mentioned Yitzchak and Rivka's displeasure with Esav's wives. The *pshat*, on the other hand, is based on the verse being an introduction to the story of the blessings. Rashi brought the *drash* before the *pshat* because it is based on what came before while the *pshat* is based on what follows.

Example no. 5

This example comes from parashat Kedoshim; it refers to laws relevant to court cases.

VAYIKRA 19:15

לֹא־תַעֲשׂוּ עָוֶל בַּמִּשְׁפָּט לֹא־תִשָּׂא פְנֵי־דָל וְלֹא תֶהְדַּר פְּנֵי גָדוֹל בְּצֶדֶק תִּשְׁפֹּט עֲמִיתֶךָ:

You shall do no wrong in judgment; you shall not favor the poor and you shall not honor a great man. *With righteousness you shall judge your fellow.*

RASHI

בצדק תשפט עמיתך: כמשמעו.
דבר אחר: הוי דן את חברך לכף זכות.

With righteousness you shall judge your fellow: Just as it sounds.
Another interpretation: Judge your friend favorably.

Rashi offers two interpretations to this phrase. Why the need for two interpretations — why isn't the simple meaning adequate?

Several suggestions have been offered to answer this question. Can you suggest a way to explain Rashi's need for two separate interpretations? (See the appendix for possible answers, page 131.)

If you have answered the question you now know why the second interpretation was necessary. Now we can ask: Why do we need the first interpretation – the straightforward meaning?

It would seem that the context of these verses is that of law cases before a judge. Judging one's friend favorably is not a court case, so we certainly need the simple meaning. That is why Rashi offered us both.

We have seen that when Rashi offers two interpretations, one *pshat* and one *drash*, it is because there is something lacking in the *pshat* interpretation. When confronted with such a comment, it is often helpful to look at the commentary on Rashi called *Maskil L'David* by David Pardue, which frequently addresses this type of question.

IV. How Can We Reconcile Contradictory Comments?

This is an advanced type of question. There are times when we will see a Rashi comment and realize that his comment seems to contradict another comment he made elsewhere in the Torah. This is cause for asking how these two comments can be reconciled.

Below are some examples of this. We assume that Rashi remembered what he wrote and therefore must have had some explanation for why the two comments are not contradictory. It is our job to find the answer.

Example no. 1

The example below comes from parashat Mishpatim. The verse discusses the law and punishment for the owner of an ox that killed a man.

SHEMOT 21:30

אִם־כֹּפֶר יוּשַׁת עָלָיו וְנָתַן פִּדְיֹן נַפְשׁוֹ כְּכֹל אֲשֶׁר יוּשַׁת עָלָיו:

אִם *an atonement is put on him* he shall pay as a redemption for his life, whatever shall be assessed against him.

RASHI

אם כפר יושת עליו: אם זה אינו תלוי, והרי הוא כמו : "אם כסף תלוה" (לקמן כב:כד) לשון אשר. זה משפטו, שישיתו עליו בית דין כופר.

אִם an atonement is put on him: The word אִם here is not conditional [i.e., it does not mean "if"]. It is similar to "when you lend money" (22:24), which means "when." This is his judgment, *when* the court shall assess ransom against him.

But earlier Rashi translates the word אִם differently:

SHEMOT 20:22

וְאִם־מִזְבַּח אֲבָנִים תַּעֲשֶׂה־לִּי לֹא־תִבְנֶה אֶתְהֶן גָּזִית כִּי חַרְבְּךָ הֵנַפְתָּ עָלֶיהָ וַתְּחַלְלֶהָ:

אִם you make for Me *an altar of stone*, do not build it of hewn stones; for your sword you would have waved above it and you would have profaned it.

On this verse Rashi writes:

ואם מזבח אבנים: רבי ישמעאל אומר: כל אם ואם שבתורה רשות, חוץ משלשה:

1. "ואם מזבח אבנים תעשה לי", הרי אם זה משמש בלשון **כאשר**: כאשר תעשה לי מזבח אבנים לא תבנה אתהן גזית שהרי חובה עליך לבנות מזבח אבנים, שנאמר, "אבנים שלמות תבנה" (דברים כז:ו).
2. וכן "אם כסף תלוה" (שמות כב:כד), חובה הוא, שנאמר, "והעבט תעביטנו" (דברים טו:ח). ואף זה משמש בלשון כאשר.
3. וכן "ואם תקריב מנחת בכורים" (ויקרא ב:יד) – זו מנחת העומר, שהיא חובה.

ועל כרחך אין אם הללו תלויין, אלא ודאין, ובלשון כאשר הם משמשים.

אם an altar of stone: Rabbi Yishmael said: Every אם in the Torah is optional [means "if"] except for three:

1. "When [אם] you make for Me an altar of stone": This means "*when*" you make for Me an altar of stone do not build it of hewn stones, because it is an obligation to build an altar of stones, as it says, "You shall build [the altar] of whole stones" (Devarim 27:6).
2. And likewise "When [אם] you lend money" (Shemot 22:24): This is an obligation as it says "and you shall surely lend him" (Devarim 15:8). This also means "when."
3. Likewise "And when [אם] you offer a first fruit offering" (Vayikra 2:14). This refers to the Omer offering which is obligatory.

So you must say that these examples of אם are not conditional but rather absolute; and they are used to mean "when."

Rashi (following Rabbi Yishmael) lists the only three cases in the Torah where the word אם means "when" – but he leaves out our verse, which also uses אם to mean "when"! This Rashi comment seems to be a clear contradiction to his comment on verse 21:30.

By examining the context of the verses we can discover an answer. In the three cases which Rashi cites – אם an altar will be built, אם you lend money, אם you offer a first-fruit offering – the word אם refers to events that will all happen and it means "*when* this happens." In our verse, while the word אם also means "when" it is nevertheless conditional. See the verses before this verse:

SHEMOT 21:28–29

וְכִי־יִגַּח שׁוֹר אֶת־אִישׁ אוֹ אֶת־אִשָּׁה וָמֵת סָקוֹל יִסָּקֵל הַשּׁוֹר וְלֹא יֵאָכֵל אֶת־בְּשָׂרוֹ וּבַעַל הַשּׁוֹר נָקִי: **וְאִם שׁוֹר נַגָּח הוּא מִתְּמֹל שִׁלְשֹׁם** וְהוּעַד בִּבְעָלָיו וְלֹא יִשְׁמְרֶנּוּ וְהֵמִית אִישׁ אוֹ אִשָּׁה הַשּׁוֹר יִסָּקֵל וְגַם־בְּעָלָיו יוּמָת:

If an ox will gore a man or a woman and he shall die, the ox shall surely be stoned, its flesh may not be eaten and the owner of the ox shall be innocent. *But if* [אם] *it was an ox that gores habitually from times past,* and its owners had been warned but did not guard it and it killed a man or a woman, the ox shall be stoned and even its owners shall die.

So our verse happens *only* if the ox gored several times previously, that is, he has a record of killing. Then the owner pays "atonement money." This means that while here the word אם means "when" nevertheless it is still conditional – depending on whether the ox was a habitual gorer.

Thus Rashi (and Rabbi Yishmael) was right not to include this verse with the other three verses he cited. It is not the same and there is no contradiction in Rashi.

Example no. 2
Let us look at another apparent contradiction in Rashi.

DEVARIM 1:5

בְּעֵבֶר הַיַּרְדֵּן בְּאֶרֶץ מוֹאָב **הוֹאִיל** מֹשֶׁה בֵּאֵר אֶת־הַתּוֹרָה הַזֹּאת לֵאמֹר:

On the other side of the Jordan, in the land of Moab, Moshe *began* to explain this Torah, saying.

RASHI

הואיל: התחיל, כמו "הנה נא הואלתי" (בראשית יח:כז).

הואיל: Began, as it says, "Behold, I have begun" (Bereishit 18:27).

Rashi translates הואיל as *began* and for support of this he refers us to Bereishit 18:27. But when we look there we find something very strange. Rashi does not comment on the word's appearance in Bereishit 18:27; he does, however, comment when the word appears four verses later:

BEREISHIT 18:31

וַיֹּאמֶר הִנֵּה־נָא **הוֹאַלְתִּי** לְדַבֵּר אֶל־אֲדֹנָי אוּלַי יִמָּצְאוּן שָׁם עֶשְׂרִים וַיֹּאמֶר לֹא אַשְׁחִית בַּעֲבוּר הָעֶשְׂרִים:

And he said, "Behold, now, I have *wanted* to speak to my Lord: What if twenty are found there?" And He said, "I will not destroy [the city] for the sake of the twenty."

RASHI

הואלתי: רציתי כמו "ויואל משה" (שמות ב:כא).

הואלתי: I have wanted, as it says, "And Moshe wanted..." (Shemot 2:21).

Strange indeed! Rashi in Devarim translates the word הואיל as *began* and to support his translation he cites a verse in Bereishit where the word הואיל also appears. But he doesn't actually comment on the verse in Bereishit, and when the word appears four verses later Rashi says it means *wanted*. This is a real conundrum.

When we read the verse in Bereishit together with the verses before it the matter clears up.

BEREISHIT 18:27–31

וַיַּעַן אַבְרָהָם וַיֹּאמַר **הִנֵּה־נָא הוֹאַלְתִּי** לְדַבֵּר אֶל־אֲדֹנָי וְאָנֹכִי עָפָר וָאֵפֶר: אוּלַי יַחְסְרוּן חֲמִשִּׁים הַצַּדִּיקִם חֲמִשָּׁה הֲתַשְׁחִית בַּחֲמִשָּׁה אֶת־כָּל־הָעִיר וַיֹּאמֶר לֹא אַשְׁחִית אִם־אֶמְצָא שָׁם אַרְבָּעִים וַחֲמִשָּׁה: וַיֹּסֶף עוֹד לְדַבֵּר אֵלָיו וַיֹּאמַר אוּלַי יִמָּצְאוּן שָׁם אַרְבָּעִים וַיֹּאמֶר לֹא אֶעֱשֶׂה בַּעֲבוּר הָאַרְבָּעִים: וַיֹּאמֶר אַל־נָא יִחַר לַאדֹנָי וַאֲדַבֵּרָה אוּלַי יִמָּצְאוּן שָׁם שְׁלֹשִׁים וַיֹּאמֶר לֹא אֶעֱשֶׂה אִם־אֶמְצָא שָׁם שְׁלֹשִׁים: וַיֹּאמֶר **הִנֵּה־נָא הוֹאַלְתִּי** לְדַבֵּר אֶל־אֲדֹנָי אוּלַי יִמָּצְאוּן שָׁם עֶשְׂרִים וַיֹּאמֶר לֹא אַשְׁחִית בַּעֲבוּר הָעֶשְׂרִים:

And Avraham answered and said, "*Behold, now, I have begun* to speak to my Lord although I am just dust and ashes. What if the fifty righteous people should lack five? Would You destroy the entire city because of the five?" And He said, "I will not destroy if I find there forty-five." He continued to speak to Him and said, "What if forty are found there?" And He said, "I will not do thus for the sake of the forty." And he said, "Let not my Lord be angry and I will speak: What if thirty are found there?" And He said, "I will not do thus if I find there thirty." And he said: "*Behold, now, I have wanted* to speak to my Lord: What if twenty are found there?" And He said, "I will not destroy for the sake of the twenty."

We see that the words הנה נא הואלתי appear twice in these verses, in verses 27 and 31. It makes sense that the meaning the first time would be "I have begun," but that can't be the meaning later on in the conversation. The second time Avraham says these words they mean "I have wanted." Rashi in Devarim was referring to the words in verse 27, while Rashi in Bereishit comments on the words in verse 31 – there he says the words mean "I desire." The contradiction disappears once we see that Rashi was not referring to the words that he translates as "I desire."

Example no. 3

In the next example Rashi cites three instances of a phrase when there are actually four such phrases in the Torah. The question: Why does he ignore the fourth case?

The example comes from G-d's words to Moshe as He prepares him for death.

DEVARIM 32:48–49

וַיְדַבֵּר ה' אֶל־מֹשֶׁה בְּעֶצֶם הַיּוֹם הַזֶּה לֵאמֹר: עֲלֵה אֶל־הַר הָעֲבָרִים הַזֶּה הַר־נְבוֹ אֲשֶׁר בְּאֶרֶץ מוֹאָב אֲשֶׁר עַל־פְּנֵי יְרֵחוֹ וּרְאֵה אֶת־אֶרֶץ כְּנַעַן אֲשֶׁר אֲנִי נֹתֵן לִבְנֵי יִשְׂרָאֵל לַאֲחֻזָּה:

And Hashem spoke to Moshe on this selfsame day, saying: Go up to this Mount Haavarim, Mount Nevo which is in the land of Moav, which faces Jericho, and see the land of Canaan which I give to the Children of Israel as a possession.

RASHI, DEVARIM 32:48

וידבר ה' אל משה בעצם היום הזה: בשלשה מקומות נאמר בעצם היום הזה: נאמר בנח "בעצם היום הזה בא נח" וגו' (שם ז:יג), במראית אורו של יום. לפי שהיו בני דורו אומרים: "בכך וכך אם אנו מרגישין בו אין אנו מניחין אותו ליכנס בתיבה, ולא עוד, אלא אנו נוטלין כשילין וקרדומות ומבקעין את התיבה". אמר הקב"ה: "הריני מכניסו בחצי היום, וכל מי שיש בידו כוח למחות יבא וימחה".

And Hashem spoke to Moshe on this selfsame day: In three places [in the Torah] it says "on this selfsame day." It says it by Noach, "On this selfsame day Noach came [into the ark]" (Bereishit 7:13) – while it was daylight. Because the people at that time said, "If we sense that he [is entering the ark] we will not allow him to enter! And not only that, but we'll take hammers and axes and destroy it." So G-d said, "I'll have him enter in midday and whoever who has the power to protest, let him come and protest."

RASHI CONTINUES

במצרים נאמר "בעצם היום הזה הוציא ה'" (שמות יב:נא). לפי שהיו מצרים אומרים: "בכך וכך אם אנו מרגישין בהם אין אנו מניחים אותם לצאת, ולא עוד אלא אנו נוטלין סייפות וכלי זיין והורגין בהם". אמר הקב"ה: "הריני מוציאן בחצי היום וכל מי שיש בו כוח למחות יבא וימחה".

Also by Egypt it says, "On this selfsame day Hashem brought out [Israel]" (Shemot 12:51). Because there were Egyptians who said, "If we sense [their leaving] we won't let them leave, and not only that but we'll take weapons and kill them!" So Hashem said, "I will bring them out in midday and anyone who wants to protest, let him come and protest."

אף כאן במיתתו של משה נאמר בעצם היום הזה. לפי שהיו ישראל אומרים: "בכך וכך אם אנו מרגישין בו אין אנו מניחין אותו. אדם שהוציאנו ממצרים, וקרע לנו את הים, והוריד לנו את המן, והגיז לנו את השליו, והעלה לנו את הבאר, ונתן לנו את התורה – אין אנו מניחין אותו".
אמר הקב"ה: "הריני מכניסו בחצי היום" וכו'.

Here also by the death of Moshe it says "on this selfsame day." Because the Israelites were saying, "Such and such will we do if we sense [that he is going to die]. We won't allow it. The man who brought us out of Egypt and split the sea and brought us the manna and gave us the slav birds and gave us the well and gave us the Torah – we will not allow him [to die]." So the Holy One said, "Behold I will have him enter [death] in midday."

But there is a fourth place this phrase is used:

BEREISHIT 17:23

וַיִּקַּח אַבְרָהָם אֶת־יִשְׁמָעֵאל בְּנוֹ וְאֵת כָּל־יְלִידֵי בֵיתוֹ וְאֵת כָּל־מִקְנַת כַּסְפּוֹ כָּל־זָכָר בְּאַנְשֵׁי בֵּית אַבְרָהָם וַיָּמָל אֶת־בְּשַׂר עָרְלָתָם **בְּעֶצֶם הַיּוֹם הַזֶּה** כַּאֲשֶׁר דִּבֶּר אִתּוֹ אֱלֹקִים:

And Avraham took Yishmael his son and all those born in his household and those purchased – every male which were of the house of Avraham, he circumcised the flesh of their foreskin *on this selfsame day* as G-d had spoken to him.

RASHI

בעצם היום: בו ביום שנצטווה, ביום ולא בלילה. לא נתיירא לא מן הגויים ולא מן הלצנים, ושלא יהיו אויביו ובני דורו אומרים: "אילו ראינוהו לא הנחנוהו למול ולקיים מצוותו של מקום".

On this selfsame day: On the same day that he was commanded, by day and not by night; he did not fear the gentiles nor the scoffers, so that his enemies or his contemporaries would not say, "Had we seen him we would not have let him perform the circumcision and fulfill the mitzva of G-d."

We see that there is a fourth verse with the words "this selfsame day," which Rashi himself comments on in a similar way as he did for the other verses. Why did he cite only three and ignore this one?

One need not be conversant with the whole Torah to recognize this question. If you know the Rashi in Devarim and then come upon the verse in Bereishit the question immediately pops into your mind.

You must search for the answer – why didn't Rashi include this verse in his examples of the use of "this selfsame day"? We certainly don't expect Rashi to forget what he himself wrote!

The answer is that the three cases Rashi cites are all cases in which G-d intervenes to foil the plans of scoffers. But in the case of Avraham, it was Avraham himself, not G-d, who acted boldly to counter the scoffers. Rashi's point in his comment in Devarim was that G-d will thwart those who try to subvert His plans. The case of Avraham was not of that type, so it wasn't included.

Example no. 4

The following is another example where Rashi seems to contradict his own logic. It refers to the story of Yoseph being sent to find his brothers near Shechem.

BEREISHIT 37:15–17

וַיִּמְצָאֵהוּ אִישׁ וְהִנֵּה תֹעֶה בַּשָּׂדֶה וַיִּשְׁאָלֵהוּ הָאִישׁ לֵאמֹר מַה־תְּבַקֵּשׁ: וַיֹּאמֶר אֶת אַחַי אָנֹכִי מְבַקֵּשׁ הַגִּידָה־נָּא לִי אֵיפֹה הֵם רֹעִים: וַיֹּאמֶר הָאִישׁ נָסְעוּ מִזֶּה כִּי שָׁמַעְתִּי אֹמְרִים **נֵלְכָה דֹּתָיְנָה** וַיֵּלֶךְ יוֹסֵף אַחַר אֶחָיו וַיִּמְצָאֵם בְּדֹתָן:

And a man found him as he was lost in the field and the man asked him, "What are you looking for?" And he said, "I seek my brothers; please tell me where are they shepherding." And the man said, "They traveled from here. I heard them say, *Let us go to Dotan.*" And Yoseph went after his brothers and he found them in Dotan.

RASHI, BEREISHIT 37:17

נלכה דתינה: לבקש לך נכלי דתות שימיתוך בהם. ולפי פשוטו שם מקום הוא, ואין מקרא יוצא מדי פשוטו.

Let us go to Dotan: To seek lawful [*dottot*] pretexts concerning you so they can kill you. But according to *pshat* it [Dotan] is the name of a place, and Scripture never loses its *pshat* meaning.

Rashi is offering two interpretations of the name Dotan. One is *drash* and one is *pshat*. Rashi clearly prefers the *pshat* interpretation of a name, meaning a name is a name and there is no need to infer any meaning to it.

Yet further on he seems to reverse himself on interpreting names of places.

BEREISHIT 38:4–5

וַתַּהַר עוֹד וַתֵּלֶד בֵּן וַתִּקְרָא אֶת־שְׁמוֹ אוֹנָן: וַתֹּסֶף עוֹד וַתֵּלֶד בֵּן וַתִּקְרָא אֶת־שְׁמוֹ שֵׁלָה וְהָיָה **בִכְזִיב** בְּלִדְתָּהּ אֹתוֹ:

And she conceived again and gave birth to a son; she called his name Onan. And she yet again conceived and gave birth to a son and she called his name Sheila; and *he was in Keziv* when she gave birth to him.

RASHI, BEREISHIT 38:5

והיה בכזיב: שם המקום. ואומר אני על שם שפסקה מלדת נקרא כזיב, לשון "היו תהיה לי כמו אכזב" (ירמיה טו:יח), "אשר לא יכזבו מימיו" (ישעיה נח:יא), **דאם לא כן מה בא להודיענו.**

And he was in Keziv: [Keziv] is the name of a place. But I say it is called that because she ceased giving birth [there]. It was therefore named "Keziv," in the sense of "Will you act towards me as a deceiver [אכזב] (Yirmiyahu 15:18), and "Whose waters will not fail" (Yeshayahu 58:11). *Because if this is not [the reason it is called Keziv], why does [the Torah] tell us this?*

Here Rashi says that the city's name must have additional meaning; otherwise the Torah would not have mentioned it. But above he preferred the straightforward *pshat* – that Dotan was simply the name of the city. Why does Rashi change his position?

Can you explain how this is not actually a contradiction? (An answer can be found in the appendix, page 131.)

Example no. 5
This example concerns the injunction not to add or subtract mitzvot. This command is repeated twice in the Torah and Rashi comments each time.

DEVARIM 4:2

לֹא תֹסִפוּ עַל הַדָּבָר אֲשֶׁר אָנֹכִי מְצַוֶּה אֶתְכֶם וְלֹא תִגְרְעוּ מִמֶּנּוּ לִשְׁמֹר אֶת מִצְוֹת ה' אֱלֹקֵיכֶם אֲשֶׁר אָנֹכִי מְצַוֶּה אֶתְכֶם:

Do not add a thing to that which I have commanded you nor you detract from it, to observe the commandments of Hashem your G-d which I command you.

RASHI

לֹא תֹסִיפוּ: כגון חמש פרשיות בתפילין חמשת מינין בלולב וחמש ציציות. וכן לא תגרעו.

Do not add: For instance, five paragraphs to the tefillin, five species for the lulav and five fringes for the tzitzit.

Rashi gives three examples of adding to mitzvot: tefillin, lulav and tzitzit. Each of these call for four items (be it paragraphs, species or fringes), and it is forbidden to add another. But when we compare this comment to Rashi's comment on the verse that repeats this command, we discover that he offers a different group of mitzvot:

DEVARIM 13:1

אֵת כָּל הַדָּבָר אֲשֶׁר אָנֹכִי מְצַוֶּה אֶתְכֶם אֹתוֹ תִשְׁמְרוּ לַעֲשׂוֹת **לֹא תֹסֵף עָלָיו** וְלֹא תִגְרַע מִמֶּנּוּ:

All that I command you, that you shall observe to perform; *do not add to it* and do not diminish from it.

RASHI

לֹא תֹסֵף עָלָיו: חמישה טוטפות בתפילין, חמישה מינין בלולב, ארבע ברכות בברכת כוהנים.

Do not add to it: Five *totaphot* in the tefillin; five species in the lulav; four blessings in the Priestly Blessing.

Here Rashi also offers three examples of adding to mitzvot, but they are not identical with those in his previous comment. The mitzvot of tefillin and lulav appear in both comments, but here the Priestly Blessing replaces the mitzva of tzitzit. Why the change?

I pondered this question for a long time until I realized that this is not a question of Rashi apparently *contradicting* himself, as is the example of the city names above. In the example of בעצם היום הזה Rashi writes that there are three cases of a particular phrase, and then apparently leaves one out – but that is not what he does here. Rather, Rashi is just giving three of many possible examples of לא תסף עליו. So our question becomes: Why does he choose different examples in each of his comments?

The best way to start our search is to look at Rashi's sources. The main source is the *Sifrei* (Re'eh, *piska* 82), which is the Midrash Halacha on Devarim. There it says:

לא תוסיף עליו: מנין שאין מוסיפים לא על **לולב** ולא על **ציצית**? תלמוד לומר, "ולא תוסיף עליו". ומנין שאם פתח לברך **ברכת כהנים** שלא יאמר, "הואיל ופתחתי לברך אומר 'ה' אלקי אבותיכם יוסיף עליכם' וגו'"? תלמוד לומר, "דבר" – אפילו דבר לא תוסיף.

Do not add to it: From where do we know that we do not add not to *lulav* nor to *tzitzit*? For the verse states, "Do not add to it." And from where do we know that if he began reciting the *Priestly Blessing*, he should not say, "Since I have begun to bless I will say, 'May Hashem, G-d of your forefathers, increase you...'"? For the verse states *"davar"* [thing; speech] – you should not even add speech.

In the *Sifrei* we have found the source for lulav, tzitzit and the

Priestly Blessing, but not for tefillin. That we find in the Talmud (*Sanhedrin* 88b):

חמש טוטפות להוסיף על דברי סופרים – חייב.

Five *totaphot*, to add to the rabbis' words – he is guilty.

But why did Rashi add tefillin to both of his comments? The command to include four parshiyot of tefillin is derived from a rabbinic *drash* rather than a direct Torah mitzva. Rashi may have wanted to emphasize that the prohibition of adding to mitzvot relates to rabbinic mitzvot as well.

Rashi may have chosen to include the Priestly Blessing in his comment on Devarim 13:1 because the verse says את כל הדבר, which is interpreted to mean any דיבור (speech) – including the Priestly Blessing.

Hopefully we have correctly understood the reason for Rashi's choices.

Appendix
Answers to Our Questions

1. Chapter 3: An Answer to the Question on Page 30 (Bamidbar 14:20)

Rashi's answer to this question is that G-d will forgive "as Moshe had said." What had Moshe said? He had said that if G-d destroys the nation as punishment for their sin, the world will say that G-d killed them because He did not have the ability to bring the nation into the Promised Land.

Rashi points out that G-d is doing precisely as Moshe had said: The nation will come into the land, so no one will doubt G-d's ability, but those that provoked G-d will be killed. That is the meaning of the word כדברך.

2. Chapter 3: An Answer to the Question on Page 31 (Bereishit 33:2)

Rashi is bothered by the Torah's word "last" in connection with Leah. She was not last in the lineup; Rachel came after her!

This is the difficulty he is dealing with and this is why he comments on these words and not on the words "Rachel and Yoseph last."

Rashi's answer is that אחרון אחרון חביב, which means "whoever is later in the lineup is more beloved." In other words, Rashi translates the word אחרונים not as "last" but as "latter" – it is a relative term. This perfectly explains why even Leah was considered "last," even though she was not last in line; she was considered אחרון

because she was further back than the maidservants – although not as far back as Rachel (who was really last and not just latter, because she was really Yaakov's most beloved wife).

3. Chapter 4: An Answer to the Question on Page 48 (Bereishit 19:6–11)

Let us first clarify the meaning of the word "opening" here. An opening refers to the opening that appears when a door is opened. We go through the opening to another room or outside when the door is open. When the door is closed, there is no opening. It's like a lap, which exists when we sit but disappears when we stand up. Likewise if the door is closed, there is no opening.

With this understanding let us look at verses 10 and 11.

> 10) And the men stretched out their hand and brought Lot to them into the house, and they *closed* the *door* (הדלת).
> 11) And the men who were in the *opening* (פתח) of the house were struck with blindness…

The implicit question is: How can there be men in the opening if the door was already closed – there is no opening when a door is closed!

How does Rashi's comment deal with this problem? He adds one word: החלל (the hollow space). He is telling us that there is a hollow space, before the door – like a vestibule, where the men were standing. This means that the word פתח does not mean opening – it means vestibule.

It is for this reason that Rashi did not make his comment earlier on verse 6, which also contains these two words:

> וַיֵּצֵא אֲלֵהֶם לוֹט הַפֶּתְחָה וְהַדֶּלֶת סָגַר אַחֲרָיו:

> And Lot went out to them towards the *opening*; and the *door* was closed after him.

In this verse, the door closed *after* Lot went out, so the problem we had in verse 11 does not exist in verse 6. There is therefore no need for Rashi to comment.

4. Chapter 8: Answers to the Question on page 115 (Vayikra 19:15)

1) This verse has several parts to it. The first says "do no wrong in judgment." If we accept the straightforward meaning of "with righteousness you shall judge your fellow" it would be redundant – doing no wrong in judgment is the same as judging righteously, so the phrase would not have added anything to our understanding. It is for this reason that Rashi seeks another interpretation.

2) The Hebrew word *amitecha* translates as "your fellow" – in the singular. (In Hebrew "your friends" in plural would have the letter *yud* before the final *chaf*.) But if the verse is speaking to a judge and telling him to judge his fellow in a law case, it should have said "your fellows" because there are always two disputants.

3) The word "fellow" (meaning, *friend*) is inappropriate for a judge and his disputants – they are not his friends!

For one or all of these reasons, Rashi added the second interpretation which concerns interpersonal relationships rather than court cases.

5. Chapter 8: An Answer to the Question on Page 125 (Bereishit 37:17 and 38:5)

The answer to the apparent contradiction in Rashi between Bereishit 37:17 and 38:5 is that the name Dotan (37:17) is essential to the story. Yoseph had to be told exactly where his brothers were; otherwise he could not find them. Therefore, the name Dotan should be accepted as being simply the name of the city. But in 38:5 the fact that the father was in Keziv when his son was born is incidental; it is not an essential piece of information. The Torah did not have to mention it; nothing would have been lost had it not been mentioned. Therefore Rashi said we must find meaning for the name Keziv; and Rashi supplied the meaning with his *drash*.

References

Elfenbein, Israel. *Teshuvot Rashi*. New York: Shulsinger Bros., 1943.
Grossman, Avraham. *Rashi* [Hebrew]. Jerusalem: Zalman Shazar, 2006.
———. *Emunot v'Dei'ot b'Olamo shel Rashi*. Alon Shvut: Tevunot, 2008.
Lifschitz, E.M. *Rashi* [Hebrew]. Jerusalem: Mossad Harav Kook, 1976.
Sarna, Nahum. *Studies in Biblical Interpretation*. Philadephia: JPS, 2000.
Shereshevsky, Esra. *Rashi: The Man and His World*. New York: Sefer Hermon, 1982.

Index of Verses Interpreted

Bereishit
Bereishit 1:1, pp. 74–75
Bereishit 1:4, p. 79
Bereishit 1:31, pp. 84–85
Bereishit 3:8, pp. 16–17
Bereishit 4:8, p. 101
Bereishit 6:13, p. 112
Bereishit 8:7–8, p. 38
Bereishit 9:6, p. 98
Bereishit 11:9, pp. 10–11
Bereishit 14:4–5, pp. 34–35
Bereishit 15:13, pp. 42–43
Bereishit 17:23, pp. 123–124
Bereishit 18:31, pp. 119–120
Bereishit 19:6–11, pp. 46–47
Bereishit 19:15, p. 53
Bereishit 24:39, p. 58
Bereishit 24:52, p. 60
Bereishit 24:62, p. 31
Bereishit 26:15–18, pp. 107–108
Bereishit 27:1, pp. 50, 113–114
Bereishit 27:45, pp. 70–71
Bereishit 30:31–35, pp. 32–34
Bereishit 32:16, pp. 78–79
Bereishit 33:2, pp. 30–31
Bereishit 34:25, pp. 88–89
Bereishit 37:15–17, pp. 124–125
Bereishit 38:5, p. 125
Bereishit 42:23, pp. 97–98
Bereishit 45:26–28, pp. 22–23
Bereishit 48:16, pp. 55–56

Shemot
Shemot 1:1, p. 75
Shemot 2:17, p. 101
Shemot 2:22, p. 43
Shemot 2:23, pp. 26–27
Shemot 6:9, pp. 17–18
Shemot 12:2, p. 111
Shemot 12:30, p. 100
Shemot 14:10, p. 68
Shemot 19:2, pp. 67–68
Shemot 20:22, pp. 116–118
Shemot 21:5–6, pp. 85–86
Shemot 21:30, p. 116
Shemot 22:20, p. 42
Shemot 22:21–23, pp. 89–90

Shemot 28:10, pp. 103–104
Shemot 32:5, pp. 18–19
Shemot 32:6, pp. 19–20
Shemot 32:32, pp. 91–92
Shemot 33:13, p. 52
Shemot 35:27, p. 103

Vayikra
Vayikra 1:1, p. 76
Vayikra 10:19, pp. 35–36
Vayikra 19:15, pp. 114–115
Vayikra 23:43, p. 93
Vayikra 26:5, p. 10
Vayikra 26:6–7, pp. 10, 105
Vayikra 26:8, pp. 65–66

Bamidbar
Bamidbar 1:1, pp. 76–77
Bamidbar 1:17, p. 102
Bamidbar 12:1, pp. 106–107
Bamidbar 14:20, p. 30
Bamidbar 15:39, pp. 44–45
Bamidbar 22:35, p. 61

Devarim
Devarim 1:1, p. 77
Devarim 1:5, p. 119
Devarim 4:2, p. 126
Devarim 13:1, pp. 126–127
Devarim 32:31, p. 40
Devarim 32:48, pp. 121–123